PURPOSE Decoded

Discover the Divine idea for your Existence and Success

Zofaa Publishing
Atlanta, Georgia

© 2015 Uyi Abraham

Write to: Dr. Uyi Abraham
P. O. Box 162766. Atlanta, GA 30321

Email: info@UyiAbraham.com
www.UyiAbraham.com

ISBN-13: 978-0692356708

ISBN-10: 0692356703

Purpose Decoded: Discover the Divine idea for your Existence and Success
All rights reserved. Printed in the United States of America

Published by
Zofaa Publishing * 1 (888) 537 5315 * www.zofaapublishing.com

No part of this publication may be reproduced, sold, emailed or transmitted in any form without the prior permission of the author except in the case of brief quotations within critical articles and reviews.

Except otherwise quoted, scripture quotations are from the New King James Version® © 1982 by Thomas Nelson, Inc. Used by permission. All rights reserved. Amplified Bible (AMP) Copyright © 1954, 1958, 1962, 1964, 1965, 1987 by The Lockman Foundation. The ESV® Bible (The Holy Bible, English Standard Version®) is adapted from the Revised Standard Version of the Bible, copyright Division of Christian Education of the National Council of the Churches of Christ in the U.S.A. All rights reserved. Scripture quotations marked (MSG) are from *The Message* by Eugene H. Peterson. © 1993, 1994, 1995, 1996, 2000. NavPress Publishing Group. Scripture quotations marked (NLT) are from *Holy Bible*, New Living Translation. © 1996, 2004, 2007. Tyndale House Publishers, Inc. All rights reserved. Scripture quotations marked (CEV) are from Contemporary English Version ® Copyright © 1995 American Bible Society. All rights reserved.
(GW) GOD'S WORD® is a copyrighted work of God's Word to the Nations. Copyright 1995 by God's Word to the Nations. All rights reserved.
Holy Bible, New International Version®, NIV® Copyright © 1973, 1978, 1984, 2011 by Biblica, Inc.® Used by permission. All rights reserved worldwide.

Dedication

I dedicate this book to the memory of Dr. Myles and Ruth Munroe and the seven others who were tragically lost on Sunday November 9th, 2014

And also to my children:
Zoe, Esosa, Joshua

Contents

I. Decoding Purpose   7

II. God Coded You   19

III. Purpose and Assignment   37

IV. The Purpose of the Anointing   47

V. The Battles of Purpose   57

VI. Purpose Partners   67

VII. Dealing with Purpose Parasites   81

VIII. Finding the Meaning of Life   89

IX. The Benefits of Discouragement   97

X. The Great Discovery   107

XI. Purpose, Vision and Success   115

XII. Purpose brings Provision   123

XIII. Releasing Purpose   129

Purpose Dictionary

Purpose is the divine idea for your existence and decoding the problems you were born to solve.

Purpose-Malfunction is when people are living outside of God's divine idea for their existence and success. This is the greatest tragedy ever known to mankind.

Purpose-Alignment: This is when you decode your purpose and discover God's divine idea for your Success and Fulfillment.

Purpose Partners are those relationships that God aligns with our lives and destinies to help us to succeed in our purpose.

Purpose Parasites are those who try to align with you to distract you from decoding your purpose.

Peer Partners are those in your circle of influence with whom you share similar ideologies, DNA and purpose.

Purpose Clarity means understanding your purpose with simplicity.

Purpose Mate is the one that God yoked up with you in marriage before you were born.

Purpose List is a purpose list that itemizes your visions, life goals, dreams and purpose.

Purpose Fulfillment is when you are in purpose and solving problems.

Purpose Provisions are the divine resources to accomplish your purpose.

Purpose Distractions are the schemes of the enemy to discourage you.

Purpose Decoded means to convert your once coded purpose into intelligible language that is understood by you.

Purpose Paranoia is when your purpose intimidates you and other people.

Purpose Makers are those who change the world! They know that their lives have no meaning until the live out their purpose.

Chapter One
DECODING PURPOSE

Your purpose is found in the specific problems that God created you to solve. You were never made or expected by God to solve every problem or to be everything to everyone. You were created by God to be the solution to some precise problems. Everything that God made was with the intention to solve a problem and add value to the existing situation or environment.

If you don't decode your purpose, you have robbed your generation of your blessing. I'm sure you already know that a Doctor's purpose is to treat sick people, while a Mechanic's purpose is to treat sick cars. When a Doctor starts treating cars and a Mechanic makes prescriptions to treat sick people, that's a **Purpose-Malfunction.** *Purpose-Malfunction* is the greatest tragedy in the world today. Purpose-Malfunction is when people are living outside of God's divine idea for their existence and success. This is the greatest tragedy ever known to mankind.

My assignment is to bring you into **Purpose-Alignment:** This is when you decode your purpose and discover God's divine idea for your Success and Fulfillment.

The greatest TRAGEDY ever known to mankind is not Ebola, not HIV, not the 2008 recession. It's Purpose-Malfunction.

This is why princes are living like paupers. The answer to "Purpose-Malfunction" is PURPOSE-ALIGNMENT

You were coded for first class living. I know that might sound cheesy but it's so true. Royalty is inside of you. God has planned for you to live a wonderful, blessed, electrifying and productive life. Your purpose is not your personal undertaking, it's God's divine idea for your existence. Purpose can also be seen as the reason that God created you. God never wasted any creation. You were not born to merely exist but to live out a set divine plan.

The concept of purpose is so transformational. Your purpose determines your friendships and those who you allow into your life. There needs to be Purpose-Alignment for relationships to be maximized.

You've been told that God had a purpose for your life. You've read books, attended seminars, probably consulted a psychic or a prophet, and yet you feel like you haven't fully grasped God's purpose for your life. I like to submit to you that the reason you haven't discovered your purpose is because you have probably been searching for it the wrong way.

You probably have been told the same purpose jargons that have been popularized by bestselling authors and speakers across the globe. They say the clues to discovering your purpose is to (i) find what you like, (ii) pay attention to your passions, (iii) fast for three days, (iv) find your prominent gifts and talents or (v) search for and follow your pain. Maybe you've believed one or two of the ideas postulated by these "purpose gurus" and gave it a try only to find out that you were more frustrated than when you first began.

I wrote this book to help you to solve the purpose problem. Let me first state that Purpose is not in what you do; it's in who you are meant to be. This book helps to lead and guide you to solve the problems that you were born to solve.

It could be something as simple as providing a smile to a customer that walks into the door at the restaurant that you work in. **You don't need a huge platform to be purposeful in your living.** Just a simple smile can add value to someone's day!

God has better things to do than to create you to fail or live out a mediocre, unexciting and fruitless life. God doesn't waste His time and so He didn't waste His time forming you and coding your purpose. Wake up sleeping Giant from your slumber and stand in your divine inheritances and purpose!

Purpose Decoded: *Purpose is not something you find, it's what finds you.*

Go for the Big life

Your existence is so divine and epic in nature that your potential for greatness is unlimited. Your purpose is greater than your experiences. Maybe somebody told you what you could or couldn't do, or they told you what you could or couldn't have. I can tell you right now that they lied to you. They have no clue who you are and why you were sent to the earth. Your purpose in life originated in the mind and plan of God millions of years before you were born. Go for the big life. Enlarge your thinking and mindset. Dream humongous dreams that baffle your mind.

Living on purpose starts from understanding the thought that was in the mind of God before you were born. The thought that was on God's mind about you was the only reason you were born. God created you to solve problems in the world- to add value to humanity – to make the world a better and happier place. *Your purpose in life is not for you to live for yourself but to live fully submitted to God's original thought for your existence.*

This thought was so awesome that when you were in sperm form, there were millions of other sperm fighting to take your place and fertilize your mother's ovary- and yet God chose you. They trembled at how amazing and awesome your life is called to be. Your birth meant the world will never be the same! Amen!

Your provision is hidden in your purpose. Stop struggling. Decode your Purpose and fulfill the divine Idea for your Existence and Success!

Purpose starts with God

Your purpose is an unraveling of an epic idea born in the soul of God. You're on earth for an assignment by God and for God. Your purpose in life is far grander than your personal achievements and accolades. Your accomplishments in life are futile if you're not in purpose. You're here to do his will and exercise his mandate. God gave you gifts, talents and passions to complement your purpose but your gifts are not your purpose.

Paul wrote in the scriptures, *"For we are God's masterpiece. He has created us anew in Christ Jesus, so we can do the good things he planned for us long ago."* Ephesians 2:10 (NLT)

You were formed by God to relieve the world of some pain. God completely planned your life out even before your parents were born to provide answers to some problems and add value to the world and in doing so you'll find fulfillment and success.

It is impossible to find purpose outside of God. Everything is centered on God who created the whole world and the millions of species living within it. *One of the greatest tests of purpose is daily fulfillment and joy.*

The search for the purpose of life has puzzled people for thousands of years. Many have resulted to invent their own sense of purpose. Purpose begins with God. We didn't form ourselves so we're not authorized to create a path for our lives without consulting with our Maker. Allow God to show you the path He has already carved out for you. Like a master woodcarver, He has the chisel in His hand and wisely creates the impressions from His mind in wood for the world to see and emulate. The bible says, *"I will praise You, for I am fearfully and wonderfully made; Marvelous are Your works, and that my soul knows very well."* Psalms 139:14

He is the perfection of beauty. If you want to have a life of Significance, ask God to reveal to you His purpose for your life.

It's really that simple. *"If any of you is deficient in wisdom, let him ask of the giving God [Who gives] to everyone liberally and ungrudgingly, without reproach or faultfinding and it will be given him."* James 1:5 (AMP)

God has not left us guessing about our reason for existence. He has not left us in the dark. *His Spirit* is there to lead us and *His Word* is there to guide us. So for you to know your purpose you need the Holy Spirit and the Word of God. With those two combinations working in your life you can never miss it. You will be equipped to win every battle that comes your way and slay any Giant in your path.

There's no Purpose without a Problem

Purpose is not necessary until there is a problem. Problems are not what we often think they are. We're often scared of problems. We tend to run the opposite direction of problems. We erroneously see problems as hindrances and they are not. What we call problems are actually opportunities for purpose manifestations. Your purpose will infinitely solve a problem. You need problems. Problems help to reveal your purpose. **There's no purpose without a problem and no problem without a purpose.**

I'm going to prove this to you. If David never had a problem named Goliath, he would never have become King of Israel. If Israel never had a problem called Goliath, David's purpose would never have been revealed to his generation. When Goliath was threatening and cussing and making grown Israelite soldiers pee in their undergarments out of fear, God already had a solution in mind called David. King Saul and the Israel soldiers saw Goliath as a problem but God saw him as an opportunity for David's true purpose to be revealed to the kingdom. It's important to note that prior to David's Goliath encounter, he was only known as a Shepherd boy. His father Jesse believed that David's purpose was to just be a shepherd boy.

There's somebody reading this page right now that people have erroneously concluded on what they thought your purpose was. They have limited their view of you based on some problems you were dealing with, not knowing that those problems were actually a set up for your purpose to be revealed. And just like David, you're going to knock down Goliath because in your purpose DNA- you're a Giant Slayer.

I've got to tell you this: the bigger the problems you solve, the bigger purpose reward you get. See, when David killed the lion and the bear (those were small problems), but when he tackled and eliminated Goliath (big problem), he became King. Not only did David become King, he also married the King's beautiful daughter, lived in the palace tax free and in a matter of years, he became King as well. Purpose rewards are endless.

Please stop looking at your life as meaningless. Don't buy into the lies of the devil working hard night and day to make you believe that your life and purpose are insignificant.

If there was nothing in you to bless the world with, I guarantee you that you would have never been born.

Allow me to tell you more about the story of David, the least likely to succeed in his family:
David was just an ordinary young man with a God-sized purpose for his life. He was the youngest of eight sons born into a middle class family of the tribe of Judah. His father's name was Jesse. Jesse was the son of Obed and the grandson of Ruth and of Boaz. He lived in Bethlehem. He was a farmer, breeder, owner of sheep and named in the genealogy of Jesus. The story of David is recounted in scriptures in *1 Samuel, 2 Samuel, 1 Kings* and *1 Chronicles*.

The story of David shows how God can use ordinary things to accomplish extraordinary feats. David understood quite early in life that God had a special purpose in his life even though the world around him didn't recognize it. He lived to be all that God created him to be. He decoded the purpose of God for his life. **If you're going to be successful according to God's standard, you'll have to decode God's purpose for your life.** The call of God for all of our lives is for us to impact the world around us and make it better. You're a star for God. Luke wrote in the book of Acts, *"For David, after he had served God's will and purpose and counsel in his own generation, fell asleep [in death] and was buried among his forefathers, and he did see corruption and undergo putrefaction and dissolution [of the grave]."* Acts 13:36 (AMP)

Purpose Decoded: *Your purpose in life is not something that you invent; it's something that God alone can reveal to you.*
David won the battle of purpose before he engaged in battle with Goliath. The greatest of all battles that anyone striving for meaning will have to conquer is the battle of purpose. Your purpose is the reason for your existence. God put it in you before you were fully formed in your mother's womb. Paul wrote, *"Just as He chose us in Him before the foundation of the world, that we should be holy and without blame before Him in love."* Ephesians 1:4

Thinking Differently about Purpose

Everything created serves a purpose. God didn't create anything by chance or accident. Nothing was set to waste. Every episode in your life is divinely scripted to advantage you. The positive as well as negative experiences all serve a purpose in our lives to prepare us for an enduring life of Significance. When we understand this reality, life has a new meaning. I want you to know that you're destined to be a superstar- a world changer. Dream big, accomplish greater things.

God said in His word, *"For as he thinks in his heart, so is he. "Eat and drink!" he says to you, But his heart is not with you."* Proverbs 23:7 (NKJV)

Most people in society seek to equate meaning and purpose with the improper measurements such as:

- Accolades - More people are seeking for titles and recognitions rather than relevance
- Achievements - performance and achievement is where many find their value
- Financial Wealth - Financial prosperity should not be confused with purpose. That can come because of purpose but it is not purpose within itself
- Relationships –they believe meaning in life is based upon who they know or the kind of relationships they have
- Family- some believe purpose is found in having a spouse and children
- People's acceptance –some find meaning from what others think of them or how they want to be perceived
- Careers – A lot of people derive their purpose and identity from their work, careers and professions
- Enjoyment Syndrome –Most people believe that the ultimate goal in life is to work hard to be able to play hard and that becomes their purpose

Thinking Differently about Problems

"When they cast thee down, thou shalt say, There is lifting up; And the humble person he will save." Job 22:29 (ASV)

The assignments for your life are *the problems you were created to solve*. Like I told you earlier, purpose is revealed during crises. We would never have known the purpose of God for Dr. Martin Luther King Jr., if Rosa Parks didn't sit on the bus and thereby created a crisis that propelled him to purpose and relevance. Problems are not what we often think they are. A purposeful person embraces problems when they come, he/she doesn't hide from it. To be successful in life, you'll need to ask yourself some of these questions:
- What are the problems I was created to solve?
- How does my solving those problems make the world a better place?
- Am I currently solving the right problems?
- Am I busy solving somebody else's assignment and not mine?
- Am I currently solving the problems that give me the greatest rewards for my potentials?
- Am I experiencing daily fulfillment and joy?
- Do I love and enjoy solving the problems I am currently solving?

If you honestly answered NO to at least 4 of the questions above, you're probably experiencing Purpose-Malfunction. But don't worry, this book will help you to decode your purpose and lead you into your divine destiny.

Purpose Decoded: *The assignment for your life are the problems you were created to solve.*

Solving the right problems

Within your purpose is everything that you need for life and posterity. The scripture says, *"By his divine power, God has given us everything we need for living a godly life. We have received all of this by coming to know him, the one who called us to himself by means of his marvelous glory and excellence."* 2 Peter 1:3 (NLT)

If you're not satisfied with your current status in life, business, finances or ministry; you can change your status by *changing the problems that you solve. People are often broke because they are not solving the right problems, which are the ones they were born to solve.*
      Let me give you a personal example. There was a time I was going through a difficult time in my finances and ministry because I was trying to be who I am not. I was too afraid to live out my purpose because I was concerned about how I will be attacked and ridiculed. The result of that was what often happens when there is a Purpose-Malfunction – lack, sadness, mediocrity and unfulfillment. After a season of wrestling with God's epic idea for my life, I finally succumbed to it. I can testify that since I aligned with my purpose and started solving the right problems, I've seen a divine turn around in my finances, businesses and ministry success. I pray the same for you in Jesus name. Amen!
      Purpose Decoded: *People are often broke because they are not solving the problems that align with their purpose.*

Driven by Purpose

I pray that you start living a life that's driven by purpose. You have to receive this mentality whole heartedly. Since you were born you were told the opposite of who you really are. But God is saying the opposite of what society says. Believe God and experience unlimited greatness.

Discussion Questions

1. Have you decoded God's purpose for your life?

2. Explain God's purpose for your life?

3. What are some of the problems that God created you to solve?

4. How does your solving those problems make the world a better place?

5. "Your purpose starts with God." What is your understanding of this statement?

6. In what areas of your life do you need to think bigger?

7. What kind of people do you believe you are assigned to?

8. Purpose-Malfunction is what?

9. Purpose-Alignment is what?

10. Are you driven by purpose? If not, how can you start living by your purpose?

Chapter Two

GOD CODED YOU

When you catch up with the divine idea for your existence, your purpose is revealed and the whole earth is *never the same*. Before the beginning began, God chose your life and purpose and coded you in a very distinct way that aligns with your purpose. I'm sure you have heard it said that you're not a product of chance or accident. It's a true statement. God wired you in such a way that when you are in purpose you come alive. Nothing makes you come alive like when you are walking in purpose. The reason for this is because you were coded and wired by God to respond to certain internal and external stimuli that correspond with who you are and the problems you were created to solve. The bible records, *"Before I formed you in the womb, I knew you. Before you were born, I set you apart for my holy purpose. I appointed you to be a prophet to the nations."* Jeremiah 1:5

You Come Alive in Purpose

I remember some time ago, I was getting ready to teach at church. I stepped on the stage and reached for my lapel microphone to turn it on. I kept trying to turn it on but it wouldn't light up or work. After some frustrating minutes I opened the battery cover only to discover that someone had put the wrong kind of batteries in it and that was why it didn't work. My particular lapel microphone will only work with Energizer batteries or a higher class battery. It will not work with a lesser brand battery type like a generic type.

I quickly corrected the problem and put the right batteries into the microphone and almost like magic, my microphone turned on and came alive. When the manufacturer made my microphone they coded it in such a way that it can only function optimally with premium batteries.

I see a parallel here with the way that God made each one of us. Some of you have been putting the wrong batteries into your life and wondering why you are not turned on. You are at the wrong job, dating the wrong person, married to the wrong person and hanging with the wrong people that are not affiliated with your purpose. You're coded by God to only respond to purpose and **Purpose-Partners**. *Purpose-Partners* are those people and relationships that God places in your life to help you to achieve your purpose.

Purpose Decoded: *You come alive when you're in purpose.*

The bible beautifully states, *"Oh yes, you shaped me first inside, then out; you formed me in my mother's womb. I thank you, High God—you're breathtaking! Body and soul, I am marvelously made! I worship in adoration—what a creation! You know me inside and out, you know every bone in my body; You know exactly how I was made, bit by bit, how I was sculpted from nothing into something. Like an open book, you watched me grow from conception to birth; all the stages of my life were spread out before you, The days of my life all prepared before I'd even lived one day.* Psalms 139:13-16 (MSG)

I come alive when I am teaching the word of God especially in the areas of success, leadership and business. I feel such an ecstasy that is indescribable. I have so much fun that would do it for free every day. But if you put me in another field or ask me to change the car oil or teach a topic on Geography, now I am out of purpose and it feels like work and a burden no matter how much time I have to study or prepare. Whereas you can wake me up at 3am and I am ready to go to flow in the areas of success, leadership and business.

Discovering what you have been called to do on the earth opens great doors for you and brings with it the greatest riches of life.

No more unfulfilled dreams

Do you have a sense of purpose in your life that you haven't achieved yet? I believe that I'm God's prophetic voice to you today. I am prophesying to you right now that your time for manifestation has come. It's time for you to go do the things that God has laid on your heart to do.

Your purpose always aligns with your passion. Have you discovered the divine idea for your birth? What is your dream in life? Do you dream about becoming a multi-millionaire? Do you have a vision of starting your own university or bible college? Do you want to write a book or a novel? Have you been procrastinating about going back to school to finish your degree? What about the nagging urge to open up a salon or a boutique? Maybe your dream is to start a successful business so that you can give more money to your church? It doesn't matter what this vision or dream is; it's not going to happen until you do something about it. There are more talkers than doers in the world and that is why most people of the world are poor and *under purposed.*

You need to realize that God put that special purpose in you because he knew you could make it happen. God wouldn't have coded you so beautifully like He did, if He didn't give you what you needed to succeed.

I have seen very good people get so frustrated with their lives because they don't seem to know how to decode their purpose. It's a painful experience when you know that you're gifted, but your gifting is not profitable yet. It's depressing and infuriating to have a vision for years that you haven't yet seen come to pass. The bible says that, *"Hope deferred makes the heart sick, but a dream fulfilled is a tree of life."* Proverbs 13:2 NLT

Unlocking your purpose code

You were born to be distinct and different. You'll never be fulfilled trying to fit in and be normal like everybody else. *God never wanted you to be normal and that is why he never created you normal.* Your DNA and fingerprints are different and unique from anybody else. This is why you can never be successful and fulfilled copying somebody else. Your coding is too original to perform well copying someone else's code.

Your God code prevents you from being normal. No one really likes normal people because normal people are boring. Normal people are not interesting. They are not unique enough to hold our attention. Don't ever allow anyone or your life's circumstances to make you believe that you are ordinary and that you are supposed to settle for whatever you find. The devil is a liar. Sometimes our biggest obstacles to success are not from the outside but from the voices within. It's the voices from within that makes us win or defeats us. If the voice chatter in your mind is louder than the voice of God for your purpose, you're in trouble. This is why it is very important for us to daily renew our minds and perspectives about life with the word of God. The word of God is a mirror. It shows you who you really are. You can see yourself in the mirror of the word of God. The mirror of God's word will never lie to you. It will show you that you are good looking, handsome or beautiful, coded on purpose, blessed with unlimited potential and sent on assignment to this earth with uncountable resources to solve mankind's problems. The bible says, *"If you hear the message and don't obey it, you are like people who stare at themselves in a mirror and forget what they look like as soon as they leave. But you must never stop looking at the perfect law that sets you free. God will bless you in everything you do, if you listen and obey, and don't just hear and forget."* James 1:23-25 CEV

Weird on Purpose

Two years ago, I wrote a successful and yet controversial book called, "**God Wants You Rich**: Success is not for normal people, why the WEIRD make it to the top." In the book I argued that super successful people are weird in some way. They are not normal like everybody else. Mark Zuckerberg, the founder of Facebook is worth over $20 billion, yet he drives the same Honda Accord he had before he became rich. He wears the same blue jeans and grey t-shirt pretty much everyday. That's humorous and yet weird. Recently, he did a Q&A session that was written about by Andrew Trotman of The Telegraph: "Mr Zuckerberg said he owns multiple versions of the same T-shirt, as clothing, along with breakfast, is a "silly" decision he doesn't want to spend too long making. He also said that he is too busy looking after the world's largest social network. "I really want to clear my life so that I have to make as few decisions as possible about anything except how to best serve this community. "I'm in this really lucky position where I get to wake up every day and help serve more than 1billion people, and I feel like I'm not doing my job if I spend any of my energy on things that are silly or frivolous about my life, so that way I can dedicate all of my energy towards just building the best products and services."

In scriptures, John The Baptist was weird as well. He didn't care about what most people were wearing in that day and time. He was comfortably decked in camel's hair living in isolation in the wilderness eating locusts and wild honey. What a diet when he could have been slaughtering the fattest beefs just like the people of his day. But John was different and followed his calling and purpose. The bible records, *"John's clothes were woven from coarse camel hair, and he wore a leather belt around his waist. For food he ate locusts and wild honey."* Matthew 3:4 NLT

Translating the God Code

God knows you intimately in and out because he formed you. He is the reason you exist. He chose you to be his masterpiece and ambassador on the earth. He coded you for a specific assignment. The world will be incomplete without you. There's a space and identity for you in the world that is uniquely compatible with the way you were coded. The bible says, "*The LORD our God has secrets known to no one. We are not accountable for them, but we and our children are accountable forever for all that he has revealed to us, so that we may obey all the terms of these instructions.* Deuteronomy 29:29 (NLT)

Defining your purpose will help you to determine the activities that you should be involved in. Be like Jesus, He did not involve Himself in activities that contradicted His purpose on earth. Jesus' purpose was to do the will of the Father and He never did anything contrary to that purpose. In the same way, your purpose should always be to do the will of the Father. From your relationship with Jesus and the Father you will derive your assignments on earth.

Purpose is the specific reason for your existence! The first step to rise to significance and relevance in this crowded world is to understand your purpose. Until you understand and receive the purpose for your life; you cannot live a life of meaning and relevance. A life devoid of purpose is like a blind wild beast roaming about aimlessly in a dark jungle.

You're created for God's glory.

I want you to realize that God wants to bless your life more than you can imagine. He wants to use you to accomplish extraordinary things that have never been done before. When you feel like the dreams and imaginations in your heart are bigger and mightier than you, then you're on your way to achieve success because God loves underdogs. Do not roam about aimlessly through life, follow the plan of God. The Bible says, *"There is a way that seems right to a man, But its end is the way of death."* Proverbs 14:12

Purpose Decoded: *The way to follow God's AGENDA for your life is to have no personal AGENDA at all.*

How is it that so often people from such humble beginnings and devastating backgrounds manage in spite of it all to create lives that inspire us? Conversely, why do so many of those born into privileged environments with every resource for success at their fingertips, end up frustrated, under-performing and living insignificant lives? The difference is in living a life of purpose.

Spirit and Word leading into Purpose

I wrote in my bestselling book *Winning The Battle For Significance*: To discover your purpose you need the Spirit of God to confirm it to you and the Word to guide you. This is where it all begins.

1. You discover your purpose through a relationship with Jesus Christ.
2. Ask the Holy Spirit to fill you up with His wisdom and lead you daily in purpose.

A relationship with Jesus Christ

Purpose begins with having a relationship with God through His son Jesus Christ. Jesus did not come to earth to form a religion. **Christianity is not a religion but a relationship with God through Jesus Christ.** You can't have an authentic relationship with God without Jesus Christ. He died for your sins and for the sins of all mankind. There is a void in every person that only a relationship with Jesus can fill. It's not about finding religion. Knowing Jesus Christ is the source of true success, peace, purpose and fulfillment in life.

I encourage you to say this prayer aloud and mean it with all your heart; *"Father, I receive your Salvation today. Jesus I believe you died for me and rose from the dead. Be my Lord and Savior. Eradicate my past. Grant me Eternal Life. Fill me with your Holy Spirit now. Use me for your work and Glory. Thank you Father for I am Saved in Jesus name. Amen."*

Congratulations! Now you are a brand new person. Read the Bible every day. Spend time with God in prayers every day, surround yourself with other mature believers, and lastly attend a good Bible-based church. The Bible says, *"For I know the plans I have for you, says the Lord. They are plans for good and not for evil, to give you a future and a hope."* Jeremiah 29: 11 (ESV)

God Chose You

God chose you to accomplish his purpose on the earth. The first reason he created you is for you to **worship Him**. God created you to know Him and to have an intimate relationship with Him. Apostle John writes, *"We love him, because he first loved us."* 1 John 4:19

Yet we know God chose us first. He is the initiator. We respond to His invitation. Jesus said, *"You did not choose Me, but I chose you and appointed you that you should go and bear fruit, and that your fruit should remain, that whatever you ask the Father in My name He may give you"* (John 15:15-17).

Mankind's relationship with God was lost in the Garden of Eden when Adam and Eve sinned. Jesus' death on the cross, however, allows us to restore this relationship with God and to have intimate fellowship with Him.

The apostle Paul came to understand this when he said, *"I gave up all that inferior stuff so I could know Christ personally, experience his resurrection power, be a partner in his suffering, and go all the way with him to death itself."* Philippians 3:10 (MSG)

OS Hillman writes: "Establishing this relationship with God is vital to understanding your purpose. If you don't have this relationship with God, you will seek to fulfill your purpose out of wrong motives, such as fear, insecurity, pride, money, relationships, guilt or unresolved anger.

God's desire is for you to be motivated out of your love for Him; and to desire to worship Him in all that you do. As you develop your relationship with God, He will begin to reveal His purpose for your life.

Your purpose in life is chosen and ordained by God. It is not negotiable. God had a plan in mind when He allowed your spirit, which was in heaven, to come into flesh and blood and be born on earth. *"The Lord will fulfill his purpose for me"* (Psalms 138:8).

God's purpose for your life never changes, but you have to make up your mind to fulfill it. Say, Amen!

Psalms tells us that *"I have an assigned portion (purpose and destiny). LORD, you have assigned me my portion and my cup; you have made my lot secure. The boundary lines have fallen for me in pleasant places; surely I have a delightful inheritance"* (Psalms 16:5-6).

At one time in our lives, we all had a vision for the quality of life that we desire and deserve. Yet, for many of us, those dreams have become so shrouded in the frustrations and routines of daily life that we no longer make an effort to accomplish them. For far too many, the dream has dissipated, and with it so has the will to shape our destinies. Now many have lost that sense of certainty that creates the winner's edge. My burning desire is to restore your yearning for purpose. Your purpose in life is not something that you invent; it is something that you discover. Your purpose brings discipline and focus into your life.

Purpose Decoded: *If you don't know understand your purpose you will live like a pauper instead of a prince*

You are pre-ordained by God for your own unique form of greatness whether it is as an ardent student, effective minister, athlete, outstanding professional, teacher, businessperson, mother or father. The Bible says, *"For we are his workmanship, created in Christ Jesus unto good works, which God hath before ordained that we should walk in them."* Ephesians 2:10

The Place of Purpose

Your purpose started in God in heaven and you were sent on an assignment to the earth. Before you think of any plan for your life, know that God had the plans first. He's been waiting for you to awaken to His plans and purpose for your life. You're on a divine assignment to the earth. Your purpose and assignment is always to a **person, place** or **people**. You will only flourish in your place of purpose. Purpose is tied to a geographical location. There is a space and place for you to excel and flourish. Not all trees can flourish in the same type of soil. Some plants do better in some type of soil. The moment you start decoding your purpose God will begin to lead you to your place of assignment.

When my wife and I were in Dallas, Texas, we were pastoring a church in the Arlington area and then in the Irving area. We worked so hard to grow the church and touch a lot of people in the city. Our prayers and efforts didn't seem to be yielding great success, year after year. But when we relocated to Atlanta under the leading of the Holy Spirit, we started to see greater success in life and ministry. The Dallas area wasn't our place of purpose, Atlanta is. God has truly blessed us beyond our wildest dreams and aspirations.

What if I told you that the reason you aren't seeing much miracles and blessings in your life might be because you're not in your place of purpose? If you're struggling in any area of your life, could it be because you're not in your place of assignment? Or you're not solving the right problems that God place you on the earth to do? Ask God to lead you to your geographical place of destiny. That's the place to be. Do not chose a place to live based on climate or job opportunities, choose based on purpose and the leading of God.

I have some questions for you: Are you in your place of purpose? To whom are you sent? Whose tears affect you? Who do you long to protect? Whose pain do you feel?

The answers to those questions will be groundbreaking for you. There's a special place that you belong. You don't belong everywhere. You can't be a champion in the field of medicine, aerodynamics, law, physics and music all at the same time. Champions are those that are specialized in their place of assignment. A fish cannot cope without water and a tree cannot cope without soil.

Purpose Decoded: *When you are where you belong, you fear no threat from rivalries*

Nobody can compete with you when you are where God wants you to be. Money, fame and notoriety doesn't chase you down, they are waiting for you at the place of your assignment. God tells us to go to the place of purpose!

If your place of purpose is in cold Minnesota but you live in the sunny skies of Orlando, Florida; you're out of place and will not enjoy the full blessings of God. For your success to be fully manifested, you'll have to be and stay in the place God put you.

Every champion in the bible was instructed by God to their places of assignment whether it was Abraham, Isaac, Paul, Elijah, Naomi, Esther, Daniel, David or Solomon all prospered where they were sent. The Bible says, *"And there was a famine in the land, beside the first famine that was in the days of Abraham. And Isaac went unto Abimelech king of the Philistines unto Gerar. And the Lord appeared unto him, and said, Go not down into Egypt; dwell in the land which I shall tell thee of: Sojourn in this land, and I will be with thee, and will bless thee; for unto thee, and unto thy seed, I will give all these countries, and I will perform the oath which I sware unto Abraham thy father;"* Genesis 26:1-3

We all possess distinctive fingerprints, irises and voice patterns, and we have an original combination of personality traits, feelings and thoughts. We all see life through the lens of our own unique experiences, beliefs, and perspectives.

When we embrace our individuality, our gifts and talents become energized. Our authentic self has permission to shine through. When we conform in order to fit in, be accepted, and avoid rejection, we shut down and give our power away. As we learn to practice self-acceptance and honor our differences, we feel safe to be our true self. The Bible says, *"I will praise You, for I am fearfully and wonderfully made; Marvelous are Your works, And that my soul knows very well."* Psalms139:14

We all wish to be seen for who we actually are. In order for this to happen, we must first take the time to know, honor, accept, and celebrate what makes us different from others. When someone recognizes and acknowledges our true essence, we feel seen and known on a deep level.

If you don't embrace your uniqueness, you can spend your entire life striving to conform and comparing yourselves to others. By celebrating what makes you different rather than wasting time trying to be like others, you will discover your unique and special gifts. This discovery will lead you to Living Your Truth. We were all sculpted to be different and unique in our own ways, that's one of the beauties of human existence.

Mother Teresa's place of purpose

Anjezë Gonxhe Bojaxhiu (Teresa of Calcutta), commonly known as Mother Teresa was born in Albania on August 26, 1910 and lived until September 5, 1997. In her early years Agnes was fascinated by stories of the lives of missionaries and their service in Bengal and by age 12 had become convinced that she should commit herself to a religious life and serve the poor. Mother Teresa knew her purpose in life was to serve the poor and she fought the battles that tried to stop her. One of the giants that stood in her way was poverty. Ordinarily speaking, the poor cannot help the poor. But this tiny woman found a way to eliminate that challenge. When Underdogs have their backs pressed against the wall, their God given creativities are aroused and they fight until they win. The Bible says, *"Therefore I run thus: not with uncertainty. Thus I fight: not as one who beats the air."* 1 Corinthians 9:26

Here was a woman who cared so deeply that when she saw other people in pain, she also suffered. Seeing the injustice of the caste system wounded her. She discovered that when she took action to help these people, their pain disappeared, and so did hers. For Mother Teresa, the ultimate meaning of life would be found in one of the most impoverished sections of Calcutta, the City of Joy, which is swollen past the bursting point with millions of starving and diseased refugees. **I have discovered that it doesn't take a lot to make a huge difference.** Even a little smile can go a long way to make somebody's day. For her, living a life of purpose meant working through dirt, wading through knee-deep muck, sewage and filth in order to reach a filthy hut and minister to the infants and children within. The children bodies were ravaged by cholera, malaria and dysentery. She was powerfully driven by the belief that helping others out of their misery helped alleviate her own pain; that in helping them experience life in a better way—adding value to others—she would feel pleasure. She learned that putting yourself on the line for others is the highest good; it gave her a sense that her life had true meaning. Your purpose is to add value to other people's lives.

Nelson Mandela

December fifth two thousand thirteen Nelson Mandela passed away and he passed with millions of people mourning his life.

He inspired many with his life by bringing down the Giants of apartheid, institutionalized racism, poverty, and inequality by fostering racial reconciliation. Mr. Mandela changed the thinking and the mentality of people in his community, regionally and all over the world. Now people are living a greater life of freedom and liberation because he embraced his purpose and left a legacy in the world. Movies are being produced about his life and books are being written about him because he shifted the lives of so many people. This is the power of purpose.

Excuses Deactivated

We all have our excuses for why we are not walking in purpose. We need to understand that Giants are not what we think they are. Giants have more disadvantages than what appears to the natural eyes. Being an underdog has more blessings and advantages than most people realize. The decision to win is what makes people successful especially when the odds were not in their favor. I am not a fan of excuses. This is because excuses give us good reasons why we should never change.

You cannot be successful until you permanently delete the excuse button from your life. I truly believe we all have potentials on our inside. Each of us has a talent, a gift and our own bit of genius just waiting to be tapped. It might be a talent for art or music, writing or problem-solving. It might be a special way of relating to the ones you love. It might be a gift for selling, innovating or thinking about new ideas for old problems. Don't allow excuses to hold you back. Excuses are your enemy. The Bible says, *"Therefore I remind you to stir up the gift of God which is in you through the laying on of my hands."* 2 Timothy 1:6

Called to purpose

Dear Friend, God's purpose for your life is specific, colossal, service-oriented and life changing for you and for others. Here are some universal truths to the call of God on your life:

Created To Worship: You were created to worship Christ. Never forget that life is not about you. You exist for God's purposes. Let God use you to accomplish His will on the earth. The Bible says, *"They are my people—I created each of them to bring honor to me."* Isaiah 43: 7 CEV

Created To Prosper: Inside of God's purpose for your life is prosperity, so that you can finance His kingdom agenda on the earth. Everything that you need to live a fulfilling, abundant life is tied to your purpose. God wants to bless you so that you can be a blessing to others. The Bible says, *"Arise, go to Zarephath, which belongs to Sidon, and dwell there. See, I have commanded a widow there to provide for you."* 1 Kings 17:9

Created To Serve Others: When God puts a purpose inside of you He always connects others to benefit from your purpose. Your purpose will always involve you serving others and sharing the love and compassion of Jesus everywhere you go. We are called to serve others just like Jesus did and gave Himself as a ransom for many. The Bible says, *"For even the Son of Man did not come to be served, but to serve, and to give His life a ransom for many."* Mark 10:45

Discussion Questions

1. What is the translation of the God code for your life?

2. In what ways has God wired you different from others?

3. Where is your place of purpose?

4. What are some of the excuses that have held you back in your pursuit of purpose?

5. In what areas of your life do you "Come Alive? "

6. What Giants have stood in your way of purpose?

7. Do you have a personal relationship with Jesus? If not, consult a pastor or someone that can lead you to Christ.

8. What has God coded in you that your generation desperately needs?

9. Explain how this message of purpose is changing your life?

10. You are called to worship. How often do you spend quality time worshipping the Lord?

Chapter Three

PURPOSE AND ASSIGNMENT

You don't find purpose, purpose finds you. Your purpose is found in your assignment. Your assignment is the work that you're to do on the earth. There's a work that you're to do on the earth. You owe a service to humanity by virtue of your purpose and assignment.

Dead rats smell. The same goes for a purpose without an assignment. You were not designed for a mediocre life. God's grand idea for your life is not just for you to earn a paycheck. *The only thing that will satisfy you is what you were born to do – Your Assignment.* You were meant to accomplish something that no one else in the world can do.

Unfortunately, most people go through life aimlessly and never accomplished their purpose and destiny. They reduce and minimize their assignment to been comfortable and pursuing a job or business ambition.

Have you ever thought of the possibility that your life could really be special? Perhaps you have a vague sense of personal purpose and have covertly thought, "I was born to do something meaningful in life." Jethro spoke to Moses, *"Listen now to my voice; I will give you counsel, and God will be with you: Stand before God for the people, so that you may bring the* *difficulties to God. And you shall teach them the statutes and the laws, and show them <u>the way in which they must walk</u> and <u>the work they must do</u>.*" Exodus 18:19-20

The scripture above clearly states that there's a work that you must do and that work is your assignment. I am completely thrilled about sharing with you on purpose. *The way in which you must work is <u>your purpose</u> and the work you must do is <u>your assignment</u>.*

Sometimes people have a vague idea of their purpose but they do not understand their assignment. It's important to understand both. Purpose conceived you. It was the catalyst for your birth. You haven't even begun to live until you find out why you are here. This thought-provoking book reveals a new way of thinking about purpose which will empower and change your life forever. It shows the link between purpose and the problems you were sent to solve.

Purpose Decoded: *The work you are to do is the reason you exist.*

The work you are to do

Before you can understand the power of your assignment you have to first believe in your purpose. God had placed within each person a vision that is intended to give purpose and meaning to life.

A recent Gall Up poll shows that 70% of Americans hate their job. The reason why we have this high number of people who hate their job is because we have people who are doing a job instead of doing the work they are assigned to do.

I was teaching at a meeting recently where I was asking the participants, "Why do you exist?" most of them couldn't tell me. They had difficulty trying to explain their purpose in the world.

You might be wondering, "Why do I have to know my purpose and understand my assignment?" That's a good question. The reason why you need to decode your purpose and realize your potential is because that is the only way that you can do God's will on the earth, maximize the reason for your birth, enjoy true success and fulfillment in life. No employee is entitled to wages if they do a work they were never hired to do. If you're doing a work that's not your assignment, you're volunteering your life and volunteers do not get paid. Only hired employees get paid if they do the work that they were assigned. The book of Proverbs states, *"Do you see a person who is efficient in his work? He will serve kings. He will not serve unknown people."* 22:19 GW

Everyone wants to know their purpose in life. They want to understand what they were put on earth to do. A life out of purpose is a penniless life. The day you understand purpose is the day of your greatest discovery. That's when you awaken out of slumber and start living.

Merely existing is not good. Merely existing is cheating your world out of your existence. Don't rob your generation of your blessings!

Purpose means the original intent of a thing. When God created you he had something specific and special in mind. There were problems in the world that he created you to solve. You can never experience fulfillment until you solve those problems. God never made anyone to fail. He has success in mind for you. There are great victories for you to obtain and heights for you to attain.

Purpose Decoded: *You were born to do this!*

One of my assignments in life is to write books that will inspire, educate and transform lives. I can remember it as if it was yesterday, the very first time I wrote my first book. I couldn't believe I could do it. It felt like I was dreaming. I remember pinching myself as I ran as fast as I could to hug the UPS driver who looked shocked by my inexplicable excitement. I did it!
"Oh Yes I did it." I shouted and danced in my neighborhood.
"Are you Ok, Sir?" The UPS driver asked.
"Oh Yes! This feels wonderful." I cried.

I took my keys out of my pocket to burst open the brown boxes to see its contents and within a few seconds I was holding it in my hands. The feeling was like that of a father touching and beholding the face of his first child.

I had accomplished something I've always dreamt of since I was 6 years old. I started writing my first book at that age and after many years, trials and tests, I finally defeated the Giants that stood in my way and published my first book. The year was 2008 and it was titled, "Blueprint for Success."

Since 2008, I have written and published 10 books that have helped countless number of people. To God be the glory. I'm fulfilling my assignment on the earth. What is your assignment?

Four Lepers who had purpose

The story of the four lepers who changed the world has greatly inspired me. These men were outcast of the society. No one thought much of their assignment. One of my favorite Underdog stories in the bible is the story of how four purposeful lepers with sores all over their bodies put to flight a well-trained army and rescued their generation from starvation and death. The Bible tells the story of the four lepers. We don't even know their names. Their health situation was their identity. Permit me to name them, let's call them: Peter, Bentley, Mackem and George.

Here is how the Bible tells their story:
"About the same time, four men with leprosy were just outside the gate of Samaria. They said to each other, "Why should we sit here, waiting to die? There's nothing to eat in the city, so we would starve if we went inside. But if we stay out here, we will die for sure. Let's sneak over to the Syrian army camp and surrender. They might kill us, but they might not." That evening the four men got up and left for the Syrian camp.

As they walked toward the camp, the Lord caused the Syrian troops to hear what sounded like the roar of a huge cavalry. The soldiers said to each other, "Listen! The king of Israel must have hired Hittite and Egyptian troops to attack us. Let's get out of here!" So they ran out of their camp that night, leaving their tents and horses and donkeys.
When the four men with leprosy reached the edge of the Syrian camp, no one was there. They walked into one of the tents, where they ate and drank, before carrying off clothes, as well as silver and gold. They hid all this, then walked into another tent; they took what they wanted and hid it too.
They said to each other, "This isn't right. Today is a day to celebrate, and we haven't told anyone else what has happened. If we

wait until morning, we will be punished. Let's go to the king's palace right now and tell the good news."

They went back to Samaria and shouted up to the guards at the gate, "We've just come from the Syrian army camp, and all the soldiers are gone! The tents are empty, and the horses and donkeys are still tied up. We didn't see or hear anybody."
The guards reported the news to the king's palace. The king got out of bed and said to his officers, "I know what those Syrians are doing. They know we're starving, so they're hiding in the fields, hoping we will go out to look for food. When we do, they can capture us and take over our city."

One of his officers replied, "We have a few horses left—why don't we let some men take five of them and go to the Syrian camp and see what's happening? We're going to die anyway like those who have already died." They found two chariots, and the king commanded the men to find out what had happened to the Syrian troops.

The men rode as far as the Jordan River. All along the way they saw food, clothes and equipment that the Syrians had thrown away as they escaped. Then they went back to the king and told him what they had seen.

At once the people went to the Syrian camp and carried off what was left. They took so much that a large sack of flour and two large sacks of barley sold for almost nothing, just as the Lord had promised." 2 Kings 7:3-17 CEV

Purpose Decoded: *A life without purpose is worse than leprosy.*

I admire people with the courage to face hard choices, make a decision and move forward in faith. Four lepers, outcasts from society, sat at the gate of Samaria. Because of their disease, it is doubtful that anyone in the city cared what became of them. Like the rest of Samaria, these four men were starving to death. Unlike the rest of Samaria, they decided to do something besides eat bird droppings and each other. They had purpose and they had a plan.

These lepers - Peter, Bentley, Mackem and George did not sit around all day discussing and negotiating on what they like to do. The choice before them wasn't easy yet they felt the pull of their divine assignment.

Peter, Bentley, Mackem and George began by asking the most important question: "Why sit here until we die?" "What if this is our moment of purpose?" Unfortunately, most people never reach the point where they ask these questions instead they sit around and complain about their circumstances. The four lepers recognized they had two options:
a. Sit at the gate and starve to death
b. Go to the camp of the enemy peradventure they will be spared to live.

You know the story, they took the latter option and on their way to the enemy's camp, the Lord amplified their weak footsteps. The enemy's camp thought they were all about to be massacred by a mighty invasion and fled for their lives.

God worked a miracle that saved the city from starvation. God didn't use the king or his Harvard trained economists, I told you He loves to win with Underdogs. Remember that underdogs are people filled up with divine purpose but overlooked by others.

God delights in using ordinary people to accomplish great feats. He used four societal outcasts who were willing to do something different from what they have always done.

I've continued to recognize the power individuals have to change virtually anything and everything in their lives in an instant. It is my dream that this book be a wake-up call that will challenge those who are committed to living and being more to tap into their God-given power and purpose. The Bible says, *"He who walks with wise men will be wise, But the companion of fools will be destroyed."* Proverbs 13:20

Making a difference

Life is not long enough to waste any minute of it. When we invest our time wisely we can get a whole lot of results. Acting on information is much greater than the information itself. Holmes notes, "Implementation, not ideas, is the key to real success."

Consider your own life: how many great ideas have you had that you haven't implemented yet? How many of your New Year resolutions have you made to happen? We can scour business books searching for new ideas, but most of us already have all the breakthrough strategies we will ever need. What we usually lack is the actions to implement those strategies at every level. The Bible says, *"The hand of the diligent shall bear rule: but the slothful shall be under tribute."* Proverbs 12:24

Whatever God has called you to do, do it with all your might. If He called you to preach and teach His Word, make sure you do that to the best of your ability before you get sidetracked on other responsibilities.

Make a move today. Accomplish something big for God. You can do it. You are unstoppable. The tide is turning to your favor. God has placed his bet on you and you are going to accomplish something great for God. Whatever you are doing, if you give up when you meet a little resistance, you will never achieve the level of success you are capable of achieving. This book is filled with good ideas that can really make a difference in your life, business, career or destiny -but only if you follow them with passion and purpose. The Bible says, *"But be doers of the word and not hearers only, deceiving yourselves."* James 1:22

Find Your Voice

As I end this chapter, I encourage you to find your own unique voice in this noisy world. Everyday everyone is saying something. There's so much noise in the stratosphere. But God called your voice to be unique and different. Following your purpose and assignment is how you make your voice heard in the universe! Finding your voice can be quite tricky, yet I encourage you to start recording your own voice! You can't be afraid or reluctant to listen to yourself. And even watch yourself as you speak, sing, dance, instruct or do whatever it is you do. When you watch yourself you can correct and make yourself better. Get comfortable with your own voice!

Discussion Questions

1. How does your Purpose and Assignment intersect?

2. Have you discovered the work you are to do?

3. What is that work?

4. What are 5 things you need to start doing towards actualizing your purpose?

5. How many great ideas have you had that you haven't implemented yet?

6. What are the ideas that God gave you that you will start working on?

7. If you knew that you couldn't fail, how would you change the world?

8. How would you find your voice in this noisy world?

9. When was the last time that you listened to your own voice?

10. What are you going to do to get comfortable with your own voice and style?

Chapter Four

THE PURPOSE OF THE ANOINTING

In addition to understanding your purpose, you also need to understand the anointing that is on your life. The moment you make up your mind to start living on purpose the anointing on your life is activated to help you accomplish your divine destiny.

The anointing is not mysterious like some think. Many don't understand what the anointing is or how it works. I would like for you to read my book called *"The Blessing Anointing"* it will teach you a lot on what the anointing is and how it works.

Everyone born on the earth is given an anointing by which to function. The bible says about the anointing in Scripture: *"As for you, the anointing you received from Him remains in you, and you do not need anyone to teach you. But as His anointing teaches you about all things and as that anointing is real, not counterfeit—just as it has taught you, remain in Him"* 1 John 2:27

Anointing is a grace that functions easily when you're operating in your purpose and gifting. If one goes outside one's anointing and area of purpose the result is often frustration, fatigue, financial lack, weariness or spiritual lethargy. On the contrary when you're functioning in your anointing, you experience breakthroughs, innovations, divine ideas and creativities.

One area in which I have a God-given anointing is in teaching and encouraging people. I have never sought to develop such an anointing but it is so evident in my life, teachings and ministry. What many people don't know about me is that I am naturally an introvert. I enjoy quietness and being by myself a lot. I don't like to talk much and I do appreciate the company of other people who have the gift of silence. Despite being an introvert, when I am functioning in my anointing I'm like a totally different person. The love for people releases the anointing in my life. The pain and hurts of others also triggers my anointing and it is released to bring changes in their lives.

The bible says "At that time the Spirit of the LORD will come powerfully upon you, and you will prophesy with them. You will be changed into a different person." 1 Samuel 10:6 NLT

What is the Anointing?

The anointing is the *empowerment* and *enablement* of God that gives you *grace* and *ability* to do the things you couldn't have done by your own strength or merit. The anointing prospers everything in and around you and causes you to excel in all that you do.

In other words, when you have the anointing on your life, everything around you will grow, *blossom*, prosper and increase. The Prophet wrote, *"Until the Spirit is poured on us from on high. Then the wilderness will be turned into a fertile field, and the fertile field will be considered a forest."* Isaiah 32:15 GW

Where do you move naturally in your life? What do you do that you don't have to work at? Chances are that's where your anointing lies. God wants you to walk in the anointing He has given to you for His glory. The purpose of the anointing is to help you do things that are humanly impossible. Jesus walked as God, healed the sick, cast out devils, died and rose from the grave and fulfilled his purpose by the reason of the anointing.

Purpose Decoded: *The anointing empowers your purpose*

Can you imagine going with a person rushing out to a meeting and trying to drive a car without gasoline? In all honesty, that car is not going anywhere. Now that's as risky as it is for a person to try to live on purpose without the anointing. The anointing brings the supernatural hand of God upon your natural life. It causes you to experience elevation. Moses wrote, *"Blessed shall be the fruit of your body, the produce of your ground and the increase of your herds, the increase of your cattle and the offspring of your flocks. "Blessed shall be your basket and your kneading bowl. "Blessed shall you be when you come in, and blessed shall you be when you go out." Deut. 28:4-6*

Don't allow people to DRAFT or DRAG you into things that you are not ANOINTED for. Your anointing does not function when you are outside your purpose. Stay in your area of calling and your blessings are on the way.

Anointing for Promotion

Understanding your anointing will also enable you to know when you are moving in a direction away from that which God has intended for your life. "I have seen this principle happen a lot over the years. In my ministry, I have some key intercessors that support me personally. One time, I made the decision to put one of these individuals into the role of coordinating prayer for an event because she was an awesome intercessor that had a keen ability to hear God. However, I soon discovered that she was a poor networker and organizer. I had placed her in a role in which her anointing did not lay. That was a good lesson for me." writes Os Hillman. This is key for your proper promotion. The anointing is a great key for discernment and elevation.

The aroma of the Anointing

The anointing of God is a fragrance that announces your presence wherever you go. When this blessing is at work within, you can no longer be obscure. It shines a brighter light on you.

Like I told you earlier, your greatest anointing is released in your area of purpose. The anointing comes with a sweet scented aroma. The next time somebody claims to have an anointing of God on their lives, you need to go closer to them and smell them. If their claim is true you will smell the fragrance of God on them; and if their claim is not true, you wouldn't smell anything on them.

Ok now, let me explain…I don't mean a natural smell, but a spiritual one. Consider what Apostle Paul wrote, *"But thanks be to God, Who in Christ always leads us in triumph and through us spreads and makes evident the fragrance of the knowledge of God everywhere, **for WE are the sweet fragrance of Christ** (the Anointed One) which exhales unto God, discernible alike among those who are being saved and among those who are perishing: to the latter it is an aroma from death to death, a fatal* *odor, the smell of doom; to the former it is an aroma from life to life, a vital fragrance, living and fresh."* 2 Corinthians 2:14-16

Joseph didn't need to broadcast everywhere he went that he was a dream interpreter. The anointing in conjunction with his purpose drew the problems to him that he was created to solve. The coat of many colors which his father (Jacob) sewed for him is symbolic of the anointing. Anywhere Joseph went with the coat on people knew he was blessed. As a New Creation in Christ, we are wearing an invisible coat of many colors that is laced with the blessings of God.

The anointing draws out problems

I would like for you to pay close attention to the problems that shows up where you are present. This could be a clue to you on the anointing on your life and the purpose to solve them. Whatever kind of problems that shows up the most in your life or around you is clue you have the anointing to solve them.

Let's say for example, people are always falling sick around you, it's because you have an anointing to help them get well. The presence of lack and poverty around you is your opportunity to reveal your purpose in not only your prosperity but also in helping others to attain prosperity.

Mark Zuckerberg saw a problem no one else saw when he was a student at Harvard. He felt that the world needed to be better connected online and socially. Hence seeing that problem it led him to found Facebook. Today Facebook is the largest social network ever and at the time of this writing Mark is worth over 20 billion dollars. The cool thing is that $20 billion is just the reward for purpose. What about if Mark ignored the problem he was born to solve? I guarantee you there would be no Facebook and that would have cheated the world out of something that has been beneficial to millions of purpose.

What problems do you see that you're ignoring? I beg you my friend, please do not ignore your purpose and the problems you were created to solve. You have the anointing to do it and make it happen. God already guarantees your relevance. The anointing makes your life meaningful.

Everywhere Joseph was, people had a problem of needing their dreams interpreted. Of course you know why- Joseph's anointing, purpose and assignment is to be a solution to the people's dream problem and interpret their dreams. In the days of Jesus, everywhere he went sinners, sick people and those wanting to learn about the kingdom of God were attracted to him.

They were everywhere he went. Sometimes they even ambushed him just to be in His presence. They were his purpose. They were his assignment. The situation is quite different in the case of the Pharisees and Sadducees; they opposed Jesus immensely, ridiculed him and made a mockery of his assignment.

Do you know why Jesus didn't spend much time with the Sadducees and Pharisees? Because Jesus knew He wasn't sent to them! Jesus said he was sent to the sick and the lost and not to those that feel like they didn't need anything from him. Luke wrote, *"You know that God anointed Jesus from Nazareth with the Holy Spirit and with power. Jesus went everywhere and did good things, such as healing everyone who was under the devil's power. Jesus did these things because God was with him."* Acts 10:38 GW

Don't waste your Anointing

Don't waste your anointing on those that you're not sent to solve their problems. Don't hang around those who take pleasure in ridiculing you. Stay where your anointing is appreciated and celebrated. Remember I taught you on Purpose Partners. Purpose partners are those human relationships that God connects you with to help you to accomplish your purpose. No one was created to be an island to themselves. You need purpose partners in your life and not purpose haters. I wrote a chapter on purpose partners. Let's wait until we get there.

Study on the Anointing

The Hebrew word for anoint is 'mashach' and it means 'to smear with oil' and the Hebrew word for Messiah is 'Mashiach' and means Anointed One! Christ (Christos) is the Greek word for Anointed. Jesus Christ is our Anointing and only He can impart His fragrance to us. When you hug someone who has perfume on, it rubs off on you and you too become fragrant with that perfume.

Christ is the Head of His Body, we are simply members of His Body and anointed by our association and contact with Him who is our Head and Anointing.

We romance the Lord Jesus when we spend time with Him through His word, prayers and meditation; and when we leave His presence, the anointing of the Spirit remains on us.

The anointing of God is the flow of the power of the Holy Spirit within us. Every Christian has an anointing within him or her and that anointing is a sweet smelling fragrance.

In the Old Testament, the anointing ceremony of a king and priest was a one-time event. When you are anointed; that anointing stays with you. The Bible tells us that the gifts and calling of God are without repentance. In some places people are encouraged to come to the podium every week and "receive the anointing' as though they lost it. The anointing doesn't come and go. He abides forever! The bible says, *"Now He who establishes us with you in Christ and has anointed us is God, who also has sealed us and given us the Spirit in our hearts as a guarantee." 2 Corinthians 1:21-22*

The anointing has broken every yoke. We have been transformed. The bible says, *"But you have an anointing from the Holy One, and you know all things."* I John 2:20

Furthermore, we should note that Jesus was anointed with no ordinary oil. The oil that was used on Him had a special fragrance that could be smelled a long distance away. As I have said before the anointing of Christ in us should be perceived anywhere we go. We have to be really conscious of it. We cannot use to our advantage what we don't know that we have.

Purpose Decoded: *Do not underrate Joy. Joy is a force. Joy is power.*

Joy Anointing

Joy is one of the evidence that you are in purpose. Joy is an anointing. It is one of the fruits of the Holy Spirit. It's a gift of God. Joy gives light and life. One hour of experiencing the Spirit of Joy can cancel a lifetime of sickness, disease and turmoil. Paul wrote, *"But the Holy Spirit produces this kind of fruit in our lives: love, joy, peace, patience, kindness, goodness, faithfulness."* Galatians 5:22 NLT

We are pleasure-seeking creatures by nature. Joy makes you younger, smarter, more intuitive, and healthier. God has blessed us with joy. In Psalm 16:*11 "You will show me the path of life: in your presence is fullness of joy; at your right hand there are pleasures for evermore."*

The fullness of joy brings pleasures forever more. Is your joy full? This is a very important question because the scripture quoted above says that the fullness of joy creates pleasures forever more. Joy even positively affects your metabolism, hormonal balance and immune-system.

The bible says, *"Restore unto me the joy of thy salvation; and uphold me with thy free Spirit."* Psalm 51:12

The Bible also says in Isaiah 12:3 that with joy shall you draw water out of the wells of salvation. So the blessing will not work in your life if you're not in joy. Joy is the bucket that we use to draw water out of the wells of salvation. Joy has some special energy that can help us. Joy has the power to transcend barriers. When you dance with joy you break down walls and all forms of limits and constraints.

The Spirit of joy produces Shalom – peace, health, prosperity, abundance, deliverance etc. When you move toward that which is most fulfilling and life-enhancing—with joy and pleasure—healing and breakthrough follows.

Discussion Questions

1. What is your understanding of the anointing?

2. How does the anointing relate to Purpose?

3. What problems have you noticed that draws out your anointing?

4. What are the benefits of the "Joy Anointing?"

5. What fruit of the spirit do you believe would benefit you most?

6. What problems do you see that you're ignoring?

7. Do you recall a time where you felt that your anointing was tolerated and wasn't accepted or celebrated?

8. How are you keeping joy full in your life?

9. How does a lack of joy negatively affect your anointing and purpose?

10. According to this chapter of the book, in what ways can you increase the anointing on your life?

Chapter Five

THE BATTLES OF PURPOSE

There's a breathtaking purpose for your life. You're not a mistake. Your life is meant to have a meaning! Life only makes sense when you decode God's purpose for your life!

Inside of every person is the desire for something greater. There's the desire to have dominion. This desire causes us to have an insatiable taste for success and fruitfulness. It is a taste that can only be satisfied when we are able to reach the goals that God set forth for us. Every child of God is destined for the best of life. The Bible says, *"Everyone who is called by My name, Whom I have created for My glory; I have formed him, yes, I have made him."* Isaiah 43:7

In this chapter, I'm going to share with you one of the side effects of living on purpose. The moment you decode your purpose, all hell breaks loose. But don't panic it is a set up.

The devil is so scared of you decoding your purpose and because of that he will stir up all spiritual and natural oppositions to try to intimidate you into surrendering and abandoning the purpose of God for your life. This is a tactic that has always been successful for the devil. He will throw the kitchen sink at you in an effort to scare you and make you doubt your purpose.

Jesus fought the Battle of Purpose

The life of Jesus is a very important one. We learn a lot about our purpose when we study the life of Jesus. The gospel records that Jesus was baptized by his cousin John the Baptist in the river Jordan. John dipped Jesus into the water and as he came out of the water, the heavens opened and the voice of God spoke and declared Jesus to be the son of God. The scripture says that immediately he was led by the Holy Spirit into the desert to be tempted and tried. Matthew records a great battle that Jesus was engaged in for forty days after God publicly announced his purpose: *"Then Jesus was led up by the Spirit into the wilderness to be tempted by the devil. And when He had fasted forty days and forty nights, afterward He was hungry."* Matthew 4:1-2

The devil tried him with every test and battle imaginable, yet Jesus came out of the battle victorious because God was with Him. God is with you too. You are destined to win and reign over all that comes against you. No weapon formed against you shall prosper. The devil cannot do anything to stop your destiny. Infact you're unstoppable as a child of God. Battles are normal and necessary for promotion.

Now something interesting happened after Jesus left the battle, the scripture says that He returned in the power of the Holy Spirit and His fame went out all over the regions. So we see that battles are necessary for divine promotions.

Luke wrote, *"Then Jesus returned in the power of the Spirit to Galilee, and news of Him went out through all the surrounding region."* Luke 4:14

Here are some of the battles that you need to prepare for:

The Battle of Faith

Faith is putting all of your eggs in God's basket. It is total trust in God's ability to perform. The enemy will always try to make you to doubt the word of God but Faith keeps you steady in your purpose. Faith is the quiet assurance that what God says concerning you is true. We are called by God to live by faith and not by sight. It takes great faith to achieve a great purpose.

When you act on that knowledge then you are walking in the spirit of faith. When you live in faith you not only have greater momentum toward your goal, you quench every plan of the devil. Remember that the devil is afraid of your purpose and Faith is the weapon that you use to defeat him. The bible says, *"Fight the good fight of faith, lay hold on eternal life, to which you were also called and have confessed the good confession in the presence of many witnesses."* 1 Timothy 6:12

Through faith we can attune with whatever we need for growth, purpose decoding and breaking free from destructive situations and habits. Faith is what you need to achieve the impossible and do exploits. Faith in God is what keeps you when you're going through adversities in your journey of purpose. Without faith it is impossible to please God. Hebrews chapter 11 lists the giants of faith. They were men and women of God who did exploits and changed destinies through their faith. **You can change the world with your faith.** Faith moves mountains and unearth treasures. Faith makes you confident in God. May God impart into you today the spirit of faith that will carry you into your divine purpose and destiny.

The Battle of Courage

Many people never live out their purpose because they lack courage. One dictionary defined courage as "the ability to face danger, difficulty, uncertainty or pain without being overcome by fear or being deflected from a chosen course of action". Another saw it as "the quality of being brave".

I see courage as the audacity to maintain your stand no matter what comes against you. It's knowing what you stand for and being bold and fearless. The enemy of courage is fear.

Fear and discouragement keep us from doing the right thing. The scripture says that "fear has torment." Conversely, courage enables us to rise above difficulty and opposition to reach new heights and establish Impact.

Courage is grace under pressure. No one ever becomes a success without a good dose of courage. Sometimes God's purpose for our lives looks so gigantic that we sweat in our pants each time we think about it. It seems easier to give it up than to pursue it.

Please know that the God that put those huge dreams and purpose in your heart is more than able to accomplish it in you and through you. Courageous people accomplish great things in their life. Courageous people never give up. They see through the storm and envision victory on the other side.

Let's get to the point. Losing the battle of courage has inexplicable unintended consequences. The good news is that because of the influence of God in your life, you will always win. The Bible says, *"In the Messiah, in Christ, God leads us from place to place in one perpetual victory parade."* 2 Corinthians 2:14 (MSG)

The Battle of Preparation

Nobody wants half baked bread. God prepares you for purpose. When you align with God's purpose for your life, you need to allow God to prepare you for your assignment. Abraham Lincoln once said, "If you give me six hours to cut down a tree, I'll spend the first four sharpening my axe!" The foundation of any assignment is the quality of the preparation. The battle of preparation is one of the most difficult of all of the battles that people face today. This is partly because we live in a microwave society. You can easily make cake by using a coffee cup and mixing a few ingredients then popping it in for one minute and thirty seconds. That's how quickly everyone wants their preparation time for greatness to be. They want to receive a grand prophecy then the next day the total fulfillment of the prophecy.

    Here's the deal, when you receive a prophecy about your future as soon as you receive it God pours out grace for it. A specific grace for the fulfillment of that *prophecy* is released upon you so that you can begin preparing for the total fulfillment of the prophecy. You have to understand that God is not in a hurry like we are. He will release His word about you and then you will be in preparation phase until you are ready for the next level. "Oh that's too long," you may say. Yet things that endure the test of time take time to process.

Purposeful people need to appreciate preparation time. God has you in this phase for a reason so that you can be fully equipped and prepared for what is next. Jesus was born the son of God endowed with all heavenly power, authority and dominion; yet it took him 30 years of preparation to fulfill 3 years of purpose.

The Battle of Love

Choosing love instead of hate is a key to success. You are born of God. You are born of love. You are born of God's word and your Spirit has been totally recreated with divinity. Know that you reign by love just like humans breathe by oxygen. When we fully receive the Father's love, our destiny gets colorful and radiates divinity. You become a phenomenon and amazement to your world. Love power is the real power. God is love. You are love. *You can't lead if you can't love. You can't save a soul if you can't serve a soul.*

The world is small for you. Nothing is too big that you cannot achieve. Your future is programmed for signs and wonders. You can do all things through Christ who strengthens you. Love is the description of who God is and it is the essence of divinity. Love is the character of the recreated human Spirit. You have become the embodiment of God's love. The Bible says, *"For whatsoever is born of God overcomes the world: and this is the victory that overcomes the world, even our faith."* 1 John 5:4

When you received Jesus into your heart, you became a new creation. The old sinful nature was taken away and the nature of God was impacted into you. The image and likeness of God in you that has been concealed by the sin nature in you is now alive in Christ. It is so easy for you to love. Love produces great courage in our minds. The power of love transforms us. Love helps us to forgive our enemies and those who treat us bad. Nelson Mandela came out of prison after spending 27 years locked behind bars. He refused to hold grudges against those who mistreated him. Today we can all say he lived a life of purpose.

The Battle of Procrastination

Nothing slows down purpose like procrastination does. I can tell you that procrastination is a hindrance to purpose. Many incredible people never tested fulfillment and success because they procrastinated to the very end. Procrastination is a thief and a liar. It will tell you that you have a lot of time on your hand and you should sit around and wait for the "perfect opportunity" to be in purpose. The bible says, *"Work hard and become a leader; be lazy and become a slave."* Proverbs 12:24 NLT

Many of us look at our current situation and see that we are a far cry away from dominating our lives and it's usually because we keep procrastinating on our destiny. Life is not long enough to waste any minute of it. When we invest our time wisely we can get a whole lot of results. Consider your own life: how many great ideas have you had that you haven't implemented yet? How many of your New Year resolutions have you made to happen?

We can scour business books searching for new ideas but most of us already have all the breakthrough strategies we'll ever need. What we usually lack are the actions to implement those strategies at every level. *That is the result of procrastination.*

Make a move today. Accomplish something big for God. You can do it. You are unstoppable. The tide is turning to your favor. God has placed his bet on you and you are going to undertake something great for God. Whatever you are doing, if you give up when you meet a little resistance, you will never achieve the level of success you are capable of achieving. So I encourage you to start taking some purpose actions today!

The Battle of Emotions

When God coded you in purpose, He never planned for you to be led by emotions. We are called to be led by the Holy Spirit. We are told in the book of Romans 8:14 to be led by the Spirit. Our human emotions are as unstable as a boat tossed to and fro by a violent storm. If you are not careful, your emotions will try to cheat you out of your purpose. Emotions are brewed in the soulish sense realm.

God wants us to be at rest in our mind and know that all of the promises that have been given to us are for us. The more we rest in God's love, the less we will see doubt and fear. A sound mind allows you the ability to focus on your desires without wavering.

Our human emotions will always want to move us away from the will of God to follow after the desires of the flesh or things that make us 'feel good.' That is why Satan attacks us in ways that will force us to respond with our emotions. God's best for us is to have the spirit of a sound mind and not an emotion driven life. The Bible says that if we walk by the Spirit we shall not fulfill the lust of the flesh (emotion). An emotion-driven life is a dismal life. We have seen many lives messed up because they did not exercise proper discipline that comes from a sound mind. Practice managing your emotions by exhibiting the effects of a sound mind. Never act or make decisions based on impulses or mere feelings. Never make important decisions when you are experiencing H.A.L.T (Hungry, Angry, Lonely, Tired). When you feel any of those emotions, STOP and think. Luke wrote, *"Nevertheless He did not leave Himself without witness, in that He did good, gave us rain from heaven and fruitful seasons, filling our hearts with food and gladness."* Acts 14:17

The Battle of fear and spiritual warfare

Fear is the single most destructive force warring against the sons and daughters of God in their pursuit of purpose. It is a weapon that the devil uses over and over again to scare the saints away from their destiny. Fear is a spiritual warfare and Jesus defeated it on Calvary. Fear seeks to strip us of power, strip us of love and cause us to lose all sense of control of who we are. Fear robs us of our identity in Christ. The bible says, *"For God gave us a spirit not of fear but of power and love and self-control."* 2 Timothy 1:7

Multitudes of people never fulfill the call of God on their lives simply because every time they try to go forward, the devil uses fear to stop them. Is he using fear to stop you? Satan uses fear to keep people from enjoying life. Fear brings torment, according to 1 John 4:18, and you surely can't enjoy life and be tormented at the same time. I want to inspire you to take an inventory in the fear department. What are you afraid of? Are there any areas in your life that are being stifled because of fear? God wants you to decode your purpose and walk in it fearlessly! Stand boldly in Christ and make an impact on the earth. *The fear of failure is worse than failure itself.* But be strong Son or Daughter of God. You have been called for such a time as this. Follow your purpose, make your dreams happen.

Success is yours, bury your fear and celebrate your victories. Receive the conviction that your purpose is failure-proof. God has planned your triumph way before you were born. **What you are afraid of is also afraid of you.** It's your time and season. No Fear now! Go Jesus!

Discussion Questions

1. Of all the battles listed, which three are the ones that you struggle with the most?

2. What are the 3 practical steps that you can take to overcome each of those battles?

Battle 1_____
_____
_____

Battle 2_____
_____
_____

Battle 3_____
_____
_____

3. How can you maintain patience when you are going through your battle of preparation?

4. What are you afraid of the most in your pursuit of purpose?

5. Who are the four people that you need to forgive the most?
1_____
2_____
3_____
4_____

Chapter Six

PURPOSE PARTNERS

Your purpose determines your FRIENDS. Without Purpose-Alignment, relationships cannot be maximized. Your purpose requires other people to help you to realize it. The same way other people need you in order for them to fulfill their purpose as well. You were not designed by the God to fulfill it on your own. **Purpose Partners** are those relationships that God aligns with our lives and destinies to help us to succeed in our purpose.

Believe me when I tell you that there are people that are assigned to your purpose. They are purpose helpers. When God was coding your purpose he considered the people He will use to attain it. Everything and everyone you need were already created by God. When your Purpose is decoded, you'll begin to understand that God's purpose for your life is so far greater than what you could do by yourself. You'll need the participation, involvement and resources of other people to undertake it. The scripture says, *"As iron sharpens iron, so one person sharpens another."* Proverbs 27:17 NIV

Purpose partners understand your calling. These are the kinds of people that love you unconditionally. They get you. They like you. They like you for who you are and not for what you have or what you are. One purpose partner in my life is my friend, whom I will call Pastor Stephen in Houston, Texas. The way we met was nothing short of a miracle. I needed a web project done at the time and I was introduced to him by another friend, who is now a pastor as well. Pastor Stephen and I met at a local Ihop restaurant late at night and started discussing the project, God and other things.

We connected well even though at the time I didn't know he was one of my purpose partners. A few weeks after meeting him, I was in a dire financial need and didn't know what to do or who to turn to. He happened to call me and noticed that I wasn't sounding well on the phone. After some minutes of interrogation I managed to tell him that I was in a dire financial need. He offered to come and pick me up and we went for a ride. I wasn't thinking much of what was going on; I was just in a zone and the next thing I knew was that the car came to a halt at a Chase bank and he rushed to an ATM and withdrew some money and gave the cash to me. I was immediately shocked by his kindness and generosity. No one had ever blessed me with that amount of money at that time. That was the beginning of countless prayer, counsel, support and financial generosity I have enjoyed from his friendship. There are times that I have felt unworthy of his love for me, but now I know that he is fulfilling his own purpose by blessing me, because we are purpose partners and that is his assignment.

Purpose Decoded: *You don't need everyone to love you. Your purpose partners already love you.*

God has placed specific people in your life to love and to bless you. Your purpose partners are your divine helpers sent by God to you. They take pleasure in helping you to succeed. They were assigned by God to you. They were coded in purpose with you. **Purpose Partners come alive when they help you.** Trying to prevent purpose partners from helping you is like robbing them from their opportunity to accomplish the purpose for which they were born. Somebody better shout Hallelujah!

Purpose Decoded: *Purpose partnership is mutually beneficial to both parties. Everyone gains from this divine arrangement.*

God has Purpose Partners

Now this is interesting. The bible tells us that God does not exist alone. He is in divine harmony with His purpose partners. He exists in the Hebrew plural form: *Jehovah Elohim* - The Father, The Son (Jesus) and the Holy Spirit. This concept is also referred to as the Trinity. Here is what I want you to catch: For God to fulfill his own purpose for Himself on the earth, He needed His own purpose partners. He cannot fulfill his own agenda and assignment on the earth without the resources and cooperation of His purpose partners – Jesus and Holy Spirit. For the agenda of God to be complete and fully manifested, He had to send Jesus to the earth to come rescue humanity from eternal damnation and the Holy Spirit to dwell and empower believers until the end of time.

If God needed his own purpose partners, you have no choice. You need purpose partners as well.

In this scripture, we see all three members of the Holy Trinity in divine harmony: *"So wherever you go, make disciples of all nations: Baptize them in the name of the Father, and of the Son, and of the Holy Spirit."* Matthew 28:19 GW

Hear this, your purpose was not decided by God alone but by Him and His purpose patterns (Jesus and Holy Spirit).

That means that more than one entity chose your purpose. They took their time to deliberate orchestrate your life so beautifully magnificent so that it is error proof.

In this heavenly senate council, they wrote the movie of your life and carefully scripted the scenes in great detail up to the second. Then you were created and planted in your mother's womb through the purpose partnership of your dad so that you can come into the world and be a solution to somebody's purpose, pain and problems. God coded you in His own image and likeness to make a difference in the world. The bible said, *"And God said, Let us make man in our image, after our likeness: and let them have dominion over the fish of the sea, and over the fowl of the air, and over the cattle, and over all the earth, and over every creeping thing that creepeth upon the earth."* Genesis 1:26

Jesus had divine and earthly Purpose Partners

Jesus lived a perfect life because he lived on purpose. His purpose was decoded when He was twelve years old. He opened the book of the law and found a place in Isaiah were there were prophecies written about Him. Jesus stood and read Isaiah 61 before all that were present in the temple. He declared and acknowledged His divine purpose.

Please read carefully what I am about to say, Jesus, even though He was the son of God couldn't accomplish His purpose without **heavenly** and **earthly** purpose partners. God and Holy Spirit are His heavenly purpose partners and the twelve disciples were His earthly partners. Jesus by divine predisposition and wisdom chose His twelve guys to carry on His work when He left the world. Luke records, *"Now it came* *to pass in those days that He went out to the mountain to pray, and continued all night in prayer to God. And when it was day, He called His disciples to Himself; and from them He chose twelve whom He also named apostles: Simon, whom He also named Peter, and Andrew his brother; James and John; Philip and Bartholomew; Matthew and Thomas; James the son of Alphaeus, and Simon called the Zealot; Judas the son of James, and Judas Iscariot who also became a traitor."* Luke 6:12-16

Biblical Purpose Partners

Your purpose is to solve some specific problems on the earth and God divinely placed some people in your life to help you realize it. Remember purpose partners also mean helpers.

Jesus had heavenly purpose partners, and twelve earthly purpose partners called his disciples.

Paul had Timothy, Titus, Silas, Apollos, and Barnabas.

Esther had Mordecai.

Ruth had Naomi and Boaz.

David had Samuel, Saul and Jonathan.

Elijah had Elisha and the sons of prophets.

The list goes on and on. The idea is the same. When God put purpose in you, He places purpose partners in your path who have the resources and favor you need. We must decode our purpose because our fulfillment in life depends upon our becoming what we were born to be and do. No amount of accomplishment can replace the joy of purpose. Even the acclaim of others won't work. One of the greatest tragedies in life is to see purpose go untapped. "God's purpose is more important than our plans," says Dr. Myles Munroe.

21ˢᵗ Century Purpose Partners

Could you for a moment imagine the world without Apple Corporation? Ok think about that for a moment. Apple Corporation and all their groundbreaking products including the iPod, iPad, iWatch and the iPhone would not have been possible without the purpose partnership of Steve Jobs and Steve Wozniak. They were aligned to one another in the early days of Apple and they helped solve many problems in the world.

Mark Zuckerberg had purpose partners assigned to his assignment to create Facebook. Facebook is now the largest social media platform in the world with over a billion users. He would not have been able to create Facebook without the help, support and resources of his purpose partners especially the Winklevoss twins and early days financier Eduardo Saverin.

Bill Gates and Steve Ballmer's purpose partnership produced Microsoft and all of their numerous platforms and gadgets including Windows operating system that is used by billions of people worldwide.

What about the Google founders? The list goes on and on. These are just a few examples of how purpose partnerships change the world. There are many more examples of purpose partnership I can give you both in the scriptures and in the 21ˢᵗ century but I think the few examples I have given before are sufficient to buttress my point.

Purpose partners are sometimes seasonal. Some partners will only be in your life for a season and then leave to go serve somebody else's purpose. Don't fret or sweat it when that happens. God has new purpose partners He has assigned to your destiny for every season.

How to know your Purpose Partners

There are several ways to decode your purpose partners. But here are a few:

1. **They add value to your life**
Purpose partners make your life better than the way it was before the connection was made. They make your life better and enrich you in every way. When David met Jonathan, the bible said that Jonathan loved David and believed in his purpose so much that he was willing to risk his own kingship and his father's wrath to see David's kingly purpose achieved.

2. **They love you for who you are**
Purpose partners are excited about your purpose. You don't have to work hard to make them like you. They are not moved by what others dislike about you. They feel that their role in your purpose is far greater than your bad press. Purpose partners love you unconditionally.

3. **They understand your calling and purpose**
You don't have to work so hard to teach your purpose to your purpose partners. They understand you more often than other people do. They can often predict your behavior, moods and aspirations and help to make the necessary adjustments.

4. **They don't take credit for your success**
Often when a person keeps trying to take credit for your success that is a clue that they might not be your purpose partner. Purpose partners want you to shine and that gives them joy. They like to be behind the scene so you can shine.

5. They believe in you
Purpose partners are your biggest cheerleaders and supporters. They believe in your purpose and dreams. Sometimes they have more faith in your purpose than you do. They want you to succeed at all costs.

6. They don't bring drama into your life
One of the main differences between purpose partners and purpose parasites is that purpose parasites always bring drama and chaos into your life. Purpose partners are for your upliftment and they help to bring clarity into your purpose.

7. They have joy and fulfillment helping you
I remember calling one of my purpose partners to thank her for being such a blessing to me and my ministry and she was almost offended that I would take the time to do that. She let me know that she enjoys being a blessing to me.

8. They pull purpose out of you
One of their assignments in your life is to bring purpose clarity into your destiny. You living on purpose excites them and brings out the best in them. They don't come alive when you are not in purpose.

9. They elevate your destiny
Purpose partners add dimension and acceleration into your purpose. They add color to your destiny. They help you get to your higher place faster than you could go by yourself. Look around you, do you notice those relationships that always lift you higher and make you better? Purpose partners are your helpers of destiny. May God send you more of them. Amen!

10. **You can know them by spiritual revelation**
One day Jesus asked His disciples who people thought that He was. Peter responded correctly, "You are the Christ, the son of the living God." Jesus replied him, "Peter, flesh and blood have not revealed this to you except by my father." What Jesus was saying is that there are some things that you can only decode and understand by revelation and spiritual understanding. In the same way, there are some purpose partners that you can only know they're assigned to your purpose by spiritual discernment.

3 types of Purpose Partners you need

The deepest craving about the human spirit is to find a sense of significance, relevance and meaning. This internal passion is what drives people to success or failure. To decode your purpose on the earth and unleash the greatness within; you'll need a Paul (**mentor**), a Barnabas (**peer partners**) and a Timothy (**Mentee**).

A purpose mentor is a very important part of your success. You need a good mentor in your life that has gone where you need to go and can guide you there. A good mentor must understand God's purpose for your life and know the plans necessary to take you there. The super successful one's have a mentor, why shouldn't you?

Mentorship is acquiring and obtaining wisdom, knowledge and information from someone else without having to suffer the setbacks, pain, suffering, issues or time that it takes to live that person's life. Mentorship is the gateway to learning how to obtain wisdom to solve a problem. Successful people leave clues. When you're linked up with a successful person you have the opportunity to get an inside look at their lives and obtain those clues for your own benefit! A fool will rely solely on his own experiences and ability to achieve; *a wise man gleans from those who have gone before him and then blazes his own trail.*

Your earthly mentor will give you a visual as to what is possible. The Bible says, *"Now Joshua the son of Nun was full of the spirit of wisdom, for Moses had laid his hands on him; so the children of Israel heeded him, and did as the Lord had commanded Moses."* Deuteronomy 34:9

Mentorship propels you forward

Mentorship is the secret to effortless success. Jesus is the greatest Mentor of all. He is the way, the truth and the life; therefore all that we can possibly learn or become is more and more like Christ. Be a passionate protégé.

Find a good mentor and learn from them. I encourage you to ask them questions about your purpose. Do not be afraid to ask those questions that are on your heart and the ones that are bothering you. You may be surprised at the wisdom that comes forth. Every champion needs a mentor and a coach. Tiger Woods pays a coach. Kobe Bryant needs a coach to remain at the top of his game. Michael Jackson needed a voice coach. And you need a coach.

One man that has mentored me in the area of generosity and philanthropy is Mr. Strive Masiyiwa

Strive Masiyiwa was born in 1961 in Zimbabwe, which was then called Rhodesia. He is a man whose values, innovations and philanthropic work has greatly inspired me. When he was 7, his family fled the country as Ian Smith's embattled government began to crumble. The family settled in Kitwe, a city in north central Zambia known for its copper mines.

Masiyiwa's mother was an entrepreneur with interests in retail sales, small-scale farming and transportation. His father first worked in one of the nearby mines but later joined the family business.

When Mr. Strive started his telecommunications business he was the Underdog trying to survive with the big names that seemed to be enjoying the monopoly within the industry. Today he is a mega successful entrepreneur worth billions of dollars. I have read, viewed and studied everything I could find about him.

Like I said before, Mr. Masiyiwa has greatly inspired in me is the spirit of Philanthropy and solutions-based-thinking.

When God calls you to a purpose, he sends people to help you to accomplish it. One of such people is a Mentor or a Father. I do not mean biological father, but one who plays the basic functions of a father to you- *Protection, Provision, and Affirmation.*

Mentor Father

The basic functions of a mentor father are: *Protection, Provision, and Affirmation.* Purposeful people are often told they are not good enough. They are underrated all the time. But one of the benefits of having a father figure in your life is the affirmation of a father.

A father can affirm you like no one else can. God knows the inestimable value of a father's affirmation that at least twice in the Bible God affirmed Jesus Christ. Mark states, *"And a cloud came and overshadowed them; and a voice came out of the cloud, saying, "This is My beloved Son. Hear Him!"* Mark 9:7

You need a father figure who will constantly protect, provide and affirm you. The provision of a father is not necessarily material in substance but in spiritual resources, ideas, counsel and other types of intangible resources. The voice of your father is a prophetic voice. A voice of your mentor is a prophetic voice as well. The Bible says, *"And they rose early in the morning, and went forth into the wilderness of Tekoa: and as they went forth, Jehoshaphat stood and said, Hear me, O Judah, and ye inhabitants of Jerusalem; Believe in the Lord your God so shall ye be established; believe his prophets, so shall ye prosper."* 2 Chronicles 20:20

When you believe in the Lord your God you shall be established. Next, it tells us to believe His prophets. Believe the words out of His prophet's mouths and prosperity will follow you. Elijah never pursued Elisha even though Elisha was older than Elijah. Age has nothing to do with wisdom and knowledge. The anointing has nothing to do with a person's age. If you look to the flesh for a mentor you will run into problems.

Honoring your mentor

Honor is the seed for divine access. If you succeed it is partly because of whom you chose to honor. Likewise if you fail in life, it can be attributed to who you chose to dishonor.

It's impossible to receive from someone who you don't honor. Your mentor's time, assets and resources are priceless so you have to respect them. A mentor will not seek for you; you have to seek them out. I have heard from a couple of people I mentor who were waiting for me to pursue them. I have to keep explaining to them that I am not the one to pursue the relationship. It's their prerogative to reach out to me more than I do them because they need what I have to offer them.

The law of honor is a trademark of champions and Giant Slayers. Honor brings success and promotion. The bible instructs us to honor those who are in positions of authority over us and that include our mentors, pastors and father figures. Your pastor or spiritual leader can play a father figure role in your life and destiny.

Spiritual authority is important in the flow of financial prosperity. The blessing doesn't flow from down up. It flows from the head down to the body and then to the feet. Money doesn't flow up. Money flows down.

Honor is a prerequisite in the school of supernatural prosperity. You cannot graduate into your next level until you pass the test of honor. I admonish you to deliberately and habitually honor those who God has set over you in authority even when they are undeserving of honor.

Purpose Decoded: *Prosperity follows divine protocols.*

Peer Partners

When God wants to elevate you, He uses someone. He uses a human vessel. Be conscious of this fact so that you don't miss your next season. *Peer Partners* are those in your circle of influence with whom you share similar ideologies, DNA and purpose. They inspire you as you inspire them. You can learn from them and they can learn from you. "Iron sharpens iron," the bible tells us.

Sometimes your mentor might not be easily accessible to you when you need them. But you're still never alone because you have your Peer Partners to reach out to you, counsel and encourage you. Please do not ignore your Peer Partners as they are necessary for your purpose.

Purpose Decoded: *Purpose partners are sometimes seasonal. Some of them will be in your life for a season. It's ok!*

Mentees

Mentees are those that you mentor. You need a mentor and you should also find someone to mentor. There are so many people that need your leadership and mentorship. Your purpose in life is to solve someone's problems. Your mentees are those that are assigned to you by God for you to help them to attain their divine purpose. Look out around you and find those that are assigned to our purpose for you to mentor and help to climb the ladder.

Purpose Mate

When God coded your purpose he also coded the right spouse for you. You cannot marry anybody just because they are cute or attractive. Not every single person is assigned to your purpose. Believe that! Your **Purpose Mate** is the one that God yoked up with you in marriage before you were born. I've counseled countless unfilled and frustrated people who did not marry their purpose mate. If you're single and reading this section of the book, ask yourself is the person you're dating your purpose mate?

Do not marry someone that you can live with marry someone that you cannot live without. Marry someone who is constantly adding value to your life. A successful marriage depends on: (1) marrying your purpose mate (2) finding the right person and (3) being the right person.

Develop your capacity to be loved. Build your love character. Work on yourself first before you make yourself available for dating or marriage. This is where so many people miss it. They're waiting for Mr. Right or Mrs. Right to show up instead of making themselves the right one first in anticipation of their future spouse. Preparation time is never wasted time. Make it purposeful. It's who you are that you're bringing into the relationship, whether good or bad.

It's in the single phase that you discover yourself before you're discovered. It is imperative that you enjoy this phase of your life and do not allow parents, families or society to pressure or rush you out of this phase without been fully processed for dating or marriage.

God has a purpose for your singleness; you need to maximize it so you can make the best out of it. Being single is not a curse; but you'll have to make the best out of it so that when marriage happens you are fully ready for it.

Purpose mates are like a missing puzzle that when it's found, it perfectly synchs into its rightful place. God prepared someone especially for you and he/she is worth waiting for. God knew exactly what He was doing when He formed you.

A person that's high on Charisma but low on Character is a disaster waiting to happen. It's important that you know that. It's Character that sails the love boat.

Don't make the ancient mistake of thinking that a dating relationship or marriage will change anyone. Infact, marriage does not change anyone's character. It only amplifies what is already inside of them. A liar before marriage will continue to be a liar after marriage. Enough said! I am writing my next book on *Love, Sex & Dating*. It will really bless you. Get a copy from my website: **www.UyiAbraham.com**

Discussion Questions

1. Who is a purpose partner?

2. Name some of your purpose partners?

3. Who are the mentors that you have allowed to speak into your life?

4. Who is your God given 'Mentor Father?'

5. How have you chosen to honor your mentor?

6. Who are your peer partners?

7. Who are your mentees?

8. Why is it important to be married to your purpose mate?

9. Why is it important to work on yourself first before you get yoked up with your purpose mate?

10. When was the last time you prayed and asked God to send you some purpose partners?

Chapter Seven
DEALING WITH PURPOSE PARASITES

One of the interesting things about your purpose is that it will attract parasites. **Purpose Parasites** are those who try to align with you to distract you from decoding your purpose. Often times they have a malicious, diabolical intent towards you. Their pleasure is to pull you down. Anything that can hurt you is what they want. But in a fascinating way, God uses our purpose parasites to prepare us and make us better.

In actuality, we need purpose parasites in our lives just as much as we need purpose partners. They are both compulsory for your purpose. Just like scented oils attract flies, so will the anointing on your life attract trouble to you sometimes.

Have you noticed that sometimes you have people in your life who completely change on you especially after a blessing or promotion? You thought they were purpose partners but they were actually purpose parasites! They finally took off their masks and you saw them for who they really were.

Please BEWARE of PURPOSE PARASITES. Their assignment is to SUCK the life out of your Purpose. They might pretend to be friends but by their FRUITS you shall KNOW them. What I am about to say next might chuckle you like it did me: *Purpose parasites might propel you faster into your purpose than your friends can.* Another word for Purpose Parasites is "Haters."

Purpose is the master of motivation and the mother of commitment. When tribes, nations, societies, communities, friendships, marriages, clubs, churches, or countries lose their sense of purpose and significance then confusion, frustration, discouragement, disillusionment and corporate suicide-whether gradual or instant reign. This is evident in our world. The need for purpose and significance is the cause of great tragedies. Many suicides are linked to people trying to find purpose. Even mass murderers and serial killers confess of their need to find purpose and recognition. In every nation there is a generation that seems to have lost their sense of purpose. It is my prayer that this book helps to guide people in every nation back to their purpose.

Purpose Parasites can't stop you

Your purpose is secured in God. Your purpose code cannot be decoded by your enemies. The scripture says that, "Greater is He that is in you than he that is in the world."

God has a special blessing on your life and there's nothing your haters can do about it. Your life began as a brilliant thought in God's mind. Your purpose, therefore, is God's idea and cannot be hijacked by adversity. *The greater the opposition you face, the greater the purpose on your life.*

The best thing to do to purpose parasites is to ignore them and stay focused on your purpose. Their joy is to distract you from your mission. The story of Joseph in the bible is a good illustration of this truth.

One day Joseph had a dream that decoded his purpose. As soon as Joseph told his brothers his dream, they immediately turned from being purpose partners to purpose parasites. In the dream that he had dreamed he had been binding sheaves in the field, together with them and their sheaves had suddenly bowed before his own. On another occasion, Joseph told his brothers of having a dream in which the sun and the moon and eleven stars had paid their respects to him.

Joseph's purpose intimated his brothers so much that jealousy and hatred began to grow in their hearts. One day Joseph was staying home with his father while his brothers were with the flocks near Shechem. Jacob, his father, was worried about his other children so he decided to send Joseph to go and check on their welfare. They saw him coming with his beautiful coat of many colors and decided to get rid of him. When he got nearer, they captured him, stripped him of his beautiful coat and threw him into a pit. After many deliberations on what to do with him, they decided to sell him into slavery in an attempt to end his purpose.

Even though Joseph went through a tough time in slavery, nothing he encountered was strong enough to halt his purpose. He was lied on, he was ignored, he was rejected, and yet his purpose was true. At the end of the day, Joseph's purpose was finally decoded and his dream came through. His brothers were subject to him and needed him for their own survival. Joseph was elevated to the office of Prime Minister and the second in command to Pharaoh.

Here is the catch of the story; his brother's hatred of him actually helped him to purpose. Their selling him into slavery was his **Path to Purpose**. Paul rightly states, *"We know that*

God is always at work for the good of everyone who loves him. They are the ones God has chosen for his purpose." Romans 8:28 CEV
When people try to do you wrong, only if they knew that God is working behind the scenes and He is using that very same incidents to promote you.

Purpose Decoded: *Purpose exalts you over your problems.*

Purpose Obstructions are essentially promotions disguised as glitches. Here are some ways you can deal with purpose parasites:

1. **Stay Focused**

It is amazing how much life can be simpler when we all stay focused on our assignment. Staying focused helps you not to see what your adversaries are saying about you or doing to you. If your eyes are single, your whole body will be full of light.

Apostle Paul told us to run our race as skilled athletes. Skilled athletes have no time to wander about what people around them are plotting. They keep their mind and eyes on the finish line. Stay engrossed in your purpose and assignment.

2. **Ignore them**

One thing I found is that purpose parasites tend to harp on the bad things and ignore the positive stuff. It takes a lot of time, energy and resources to respond and answer to critics. You can't always pay attention to the foolishness people say or do to you.

If you think too much about it, you might find yourself believing the negative things haters say about you. Jesus was masterful at this. He didn't spend a lot of time concentrating on His critics. Learn how to ignore your adversaries and move forward with your purpose.

3. Stay in love

Choosing love instead of hate is a key to success and purpose. Nelson Mandela came out of prison after spending 27 years locked behind bars. He refused to hold grudges against those who mistreated him. When we fully receive God's love, our destiny gets colorful and radiates divinity. God is love. You are love. Love your enemies and forgive your haters.

4. Don't retaliate

When a hater hates, they're looking for a response. They want to drag you into a fight. Don't take this bait because any battle that takes you out of your purpose is detrimental to your destiny. If you retaliate, you're giving them what they want and they don't deserve your time and energy. Don't try to think of a clever comeback to humiliate them. Stay on track with God; in the end, haters always manage to humiliate themselves without any help.

5. Pray for them

Often time's people hate on others because they are really hurting on the inside. Purpose parasites can be helped and can be converted. Jesus told us to pray for our enemies and for those who despitefully use us. I understand that this might be hard to swallow. It's not easy to love and pray for those who are bent on hurting you. But you know what, God got you covered. It is important for believers to understand that his or her purpose in life is to be God's priest and intercessor for the world. The bible says, *"No curse can touch Jacob; no magic has any power against Israel. For now it will be said of Jacob, 'What wonders God has done for Israel!'"* Numbers 23:23 NLT

Discussion Questions

1. What are purpose parasites?

2. What's another for purpose parasites?

3. How have purpose parasites affected you?

4. Of the 5 ways you can deal with purpose obstructions/parasites which way do you need to capitalize on?

5. Why do you need purpose parasites?

6. What are some differences between purpose partners and purpose parasites?

7. Can you name a popular purpose parasite in the bible?

8. Why was the purpose parasite you named in Question (7) necessary?

9. Sometimes purpose parasites hurt us, who are those that you need to forgive?

10. What are the steps that you need to take to continue to stay in love?

Chapter Eight

FINDING THE MEANING OF LIFE

If you ask people, "Why do you exist?" most cannot tell you. They cannot explain their purpose in the world neither can they tell you the meaning of their life. This is a problem of catastrophic proportions. This is a problem I saw in the world and is the reason I wrote this book so that many will read and find the meaning of their lives and decode God's purpose for their birth.

You were born to solve specific problems. Your purpose is in solving the exact problems that you were created to solve and take people to a higher and better place. When you solve the right problems you were created to solve you'll experience manifold blessings and prosperity. I'd like you to know that it's impossible to be in purpose and not prosper and be blessed. Please allow me to say this again, "The only reason people suffer and lack is because they are not in their divine purpose."

Purpose Decoded: *The poorest person on the earth is the person without a divine purpose.*

It's impossible to find purpose outside of God. Everything is centered on God who created the whole world and the millions of species living in them. God decided your life before you were born. The bible says, *"You can make many plans, but the LORD's purpose will prevail."* Proverbs 19:21 NLT

The meaning of your life is to live out your purpose on the earth. **Your life is meaningless outside of your purpose.** A lack of purpose is an epidemic in the world. As I travel and teach all over the world, I have discovered that a lot of people are just going through the motions of the day. Their lives are like the hand of the clock that just goes in a circular motion every hour of the day nonstop. God spoke concerning Moses, *"But I have raised you up for this very purpose, that I might show you my power and that my name might be proclaimed in all the earth."* Exodus 9:16 NIV

The meaning of your life is to serve God in His purpose for your life. That means you do everything that He wants you to do. Knowing Jesus intimately becomes your greatest pursuit. What a glorious bliss to know Jesus intimately. He saved us so that we can serve Him and reach the world for Him. Unfortunately, we've all become so preoccupied with our own self-invented plans and ambitions that we fall short of the divine idea for our existence.

The meaning of your life is to succeed beyond your wildest dreams and imaginations. You came to be a bearer of hope to the world. God expects you to aspire to your highest aspirations.

The day I discovered the meaning of my life it sent chills down my body like a Chicago winter. I suddenly realized that my life was essentially finished before it started. My role in this glorious movie that God had meticulously scripted for me was to live it out. It blew my mind to comprehend that every scene and episode was divinely scripted to advantage me – even the good, the bad and the ugly. What a relief that brought down my sanctified soul. Now I see the world differently. I see my life with brand new eyes. When hurtful things happen to me I don't allow it to ruin my day because I understand that the situation is working out for my advantage. I rejoice and give God praise. **God never wastes a crisis.**

He uses every crisis in your life to bring you closer to your divine purpose.

Royal Dynasty

You deserve first class of everything all throughout your life. I know that might sound cheesy but it is so true. Royalty is inside of you. God has planned for you to live a wonderful, blessed, electrifying and productive life. There is no iota of failure or suffering in God's divine idea for your life. Your existence on earth is a royal one full of divine privileges. Apostle Peter writes, *But you are a chosen people, a royal priesthood, a holy nation, God's special possession, that you may declare the praises of him who called you out of darkness into his wonderful light."* 1 Peter 2:9 NIV

I encourage you today to take a stand to live a life of Significance and be all that you were created to be. I'm sure that by now you understand that you were created to be a solution to mankind's problems. Another thing that is interesting about you is that your birth was pre-planned and well thought out before you were even born. God wired you to live out divinity in your humanity. Purpose is all over you causing you to break forth on every side.

God has a special mission for you to do and you are going to need money to do it. When your heartbeat is for the propagation of the gospel and the extension of God's kingdom, kingdom wealth will naturally follow you like bees follow honey. Even the scripture says that goodness and mercy shall follow you all the days of your life.

Now you are discovering who you really are. You are born again, born anew, born of love, born into wealth and favor, blessing and honor. There is no sickness or disease in your new heritage. If you feel sick in your body, put your right hand where you hurt and boldly declare *"I am a child of God, a child of the covenant of blessing. I declare that Abraham's blessings are mine. Any sickness or disease in my body, I command you to dissolve and disappear right now in the name of Jesus! Amen! I am healed and whole! Hallelujah."*

Financial Warrior

The meaning of life is for you to prosper and propagate the kingdom of God. Money is a defense and also a weapon for offense against the wiles of the enemy. God is building an army of financial warriors that are going to be armed with the weapons of prosperity like the world has never seen before. This great army of the Lord is not going to be armed with guns and knives and physical weapons, No this army is going to be dangerously armed and equipped with the financial weaponry of prosperity to fight the last great battle of the body of Christ. They will defeat and destroy the agents of lack and poverty wherever they find it. Praise God!

God's end time army's purpose is to develop the next breakthroughs in medicine, in social media, eradicate evil and poverty in the world, innovate kingdom principles on earth, control the financial sector and force economic and military powers to bow to the Lord Jesus. They will be fearless and powerful. The bible says, "*Put on the whole armor of God, that you may be able to stand against the wiles of the devil.* Ephesians 6:11

This is a rally cry to all the sleeper cells of the Lord's army to rise up to purpose and fund the gospel.

To leave a legacy

God wants you to live out the reason for your existence so you can accomplish your dreams and assignment on the earth and leave a legacy that future generations will benefit from. If you're unsuccessful, how are you going to leave an inheritance for your children? That will not be possible if you don't have enough for your own self. Many children are born into this world and they don't start right. What I mean by that is that they start disadvantaged. I believe, based on the word of God, that this is not supposed to be. King Solomon said, "*A good man leaveth an inheritance to his children's children: and the wealth of the sinner is laid up for the just.*" Proverbs 13:22

There are two specific types of legacy that I want us to look at, the first being **spiritual legacy**. A spiritual legacy is also called a spiritual inheritance which is being able to impact future generations with an investment of eternal value. Your family, children and grandchildren should be the number one target for your spiritual legacy.

We should teach our children the way of the Lord so that when they are old they will not depart from the faith. This doesn't happen accidentally! The Psalmist said, "*Lo, children are a heritage of the Lord: and the fruit of the womb is his reward."* Psalms 127:3

As I said earlier, a good man leaves an inheritance for his children's children. You can leave durable legacy by influencing and teaching your children and grandchildren to know and serve the Lord by living a godly life and building their lives on the eternal Word of God. As your children see the spiritual and physical benefits of serving God they will be motivated to follow suit. The scripture says, *"Children's children are the crown of old men; and the glory of children are their fathers."* Proverbs 17:6

The second type of legacy is leaving a **financial legacy**. If you were to die today, how would your wife and children cope? 'You may say, "Well I don't believe in life insurance, I don't believe it's right."

But let us stop for a moment and think, if you were to have an unfortunate situation arise in your life, how would your family cope? You may say, 'well that's negative I don't want to think about that.' There is nothing wrong with thinking and planning about the future. Taking steps now while you are healthy and everything is going well is the best form of preparation that you can make for your family. You might be a woman and God is speaking to you in this scripture as well.

There is no male or female in the spirit but a new creation in Christ. See Galatians 3:26-29.

Every person whether single or married, male or female, white or black should have some sort of **life insurance**. You should also have "critical illness cover," or savings at the minimum put aside for your children or better still leave them riches and a good name. In some families children get an allowance each month. That money should not be spent by the parents but that money should be put aside in a savings account as an investment for the child. I am a big advocate of divine health and longevity. That is what the Word of God promised us, yet, divine wisdom shows us the importance of planning for unexpected events and occurrences. The bible says, *"If the iron be blunt, and he do not whet the edge, then must he put to more strength: but wisdom is profitable to direct."* Ecclesiastes 10:10

To enjoy your life

When we're in purpose we naturally enjoy our lives and what we do. God wants you to enjoy every second of your life. Be intentional in enjoying your life and purpose. Jesus already suffered for you and me so that we can live for Him. Apostle Paul said, *"Charge them that are rich in this world, that they be not highminded, nor trust in uncertain riches, but in the living God,* **who giveth** *us* **richly all things** *to enjoy."* 1 Timothy 6:17

Many people who are not enjoying their lives often are in Purpose-Malfunction. One of the symptoms of Purpose-Malfunction is the lack of pleasure and enjoyment in their lives.

They are outside of the sphere and anointing of their purpose. I shared earlier with you that the anointing of purpose brings joy into our lives. This joy allows you to enjoy your life.

Ironically there are those running around preaching the gospel of lack and suffering. They say that we are to suffer for Jesus exclusively throughout our Christian lives.

I disagree and they are wrong. The bible tells us that we will suffer persecutions for Christ sake sometimes but we will enjoy His blessings every time. God is a good God and a wonderful father who provides and pleasures in our blessings.

Discussion Questions

1. What is the meaning of your life?

2. In what ways are you going to leave a spiritual legacy?

3. In what ways will you leave a financial legacy?

4. If someone asks you, "Why do you exist?" How would you answer?

5. Are you enjoying your life or enduring your life?

6. How can you enjoy your life and purpose better?

7. Purpose brings clarity. How do you plan to bring clarity into your purpose?

8. Do you have a life insurance or plan on getting one soon?

9. What kind of problems were you born to solve?

10. How would discovering the purpose of your life change you in any way?

Chapter Nine

THE BENEFITS OF DISCOURAGEMENT

I remember many years ago when I was dating this beautiful young lady whom I will call Miss RiskyBaby. She was beautiful, intelligent and accomplished for her age. She was also in ministry and working as a secretary to her pastor who was my friend. I was so head over heels with her that I wanted her to be my wife at all costs. I foolishly thought she was going in the same direction with me in life, in ministry and in service to God and humanity. One day, out of the blue she stopped taking my calls and stopped responding to my texts. Of course you know I was devastated about that because I loved her.

I later found out she was involved with someone else and she broke off the relationship with me without any notice or courtesy. I was so devastated by her actions and how she did me. I was so hurt that I briefly contemplated suicide, mass murder etc. But you know, God would not allow those negative thoughts to bear any roots in my heart or mind. God sent me the right **Purpose Partners** in that season who prayed for me, encouraged and supported me. This is one of the reasons I believe so much in Purpose Partners.

Anyways, a few months after that, I met my wife and the love of my life, Dr. Faith Abraham. After ten years of marriage at the time of this writing, I can honestly say that she is my **Purpose Mate**. I am so glad that the other young lady disappointed me and left me so that I can truly see who my wife is. Looking back now I would have never been happy, blessed or fulfilled in marriage to Miss RiskyBaby. I later found out she was not really sold out to God like she led me and others to believe. She was out most nights drinking, partying, cussing like a sailor, snappy and contentious – that's not God's divine idea for my Purpose Mate.

The last time someone briefed me about Miss RiskyBaby she was no longer in the church but now living a worldly lifestyle. You see, all disappointments have benefits you haven't thought of yet. I pray for the Lord to open your eyes so that you can see all the negative consequences of those things and people that you thought were blessings but are really death traps.

Apostle Paul rightly states, *"And we know that God causes everything to work together for the good of those who love God and are called according to his purpose for them."* Romans 8:28 NLT

The Abilities of Disabilities

God is a master at bringing strengths out of weaknesses. When you call yourself small it is because you haven't seen the greatness that is possible with you. One thing about people I don't like is that often times, people are so quick to judge and define us. I am here sent by God to tell you today that in every disability in your life lay your true abilities. For instance, if you're experiencing financial disabilities right now, it could be that you have a gifting for prosperity and God is still training you in prosperity. After all, no Army General wants to place an untested and untrained soldier in the battle ground. Some of the greatest people that the world has ever known had profound disabilities. And in those disabilities they found their true calling and purpose. Jesus was born in a mere manger without any natural financial or social connections and yet in that limited earthly resource He learnt how to trade His earthly disabilities for the divine abilities of God.

All you have to do when you find any disability in your life, whether it is financial, emotional, economical, mental, societal or relational is to trade your disabilities for God's divine abilities. Do not allow your life to be limited to your disabilities.

Paul Orfalea was born on November 28th, 1947 in Los Angeles, California. He didn't do very well in school. His peers and teachers where often frustrated with him due to his poor report grades. According to Orfalea, in high school, his regular report card was "two C's, three D's, and an F."

He had dyslexia and attention deficit hyperactivity disorder, Orfalea allegedly flunked two grades and was expelled from several schools. But he never allowed his disabilities to handicap him.

He later attended the University of Southern California. Despite being fired from a number of jobs, he was able to gather some financial help from his family and started his own business. Later in life he remarked on the subject of his handicaps, "I get bored easily, and that is a great motivator, I think everybody should have dyslexia and ADHD."

Paul founded Kinkos which he later sold to Fedex for billions of dollars. Not too bad for someone diagnosed with disabilities. Praise God for never counting us out!

Your purpose is not limited by your struggles. I admonish you today to rise up above the struggles and lacks that are trying to suffocate your purpose like a gold fish out of water.

Make up your mind to be all you were born to be and maximize your existence. Follow God's plan and provision for your life.

Apostle Paul told the Philippians church, *"I can do all things through Christ who strengthens me."* Philippians 4:13

Thinking differently about discouragements

Discouragements are not what we usually think they are. Discouragements are the symptoms of success and progress. "What does that mean?" You might ask. I will tell you.

Discouragements are actually signs that you are succeeding. This is because only succeeding people get discouraged. When you're achieving purpose, sometimes discouragement comes in to remind you that you are not where you used to be, but you are changing to become a better person.

Someone that is not doing anything mega or major in their lives don't experience the privilege of discouragement. I will share later in this chapter, ten benefits of discouragements.

Keep on moving, don't stop

Keep on moving in spite of whatever pain, hurts, setbacks or discouragements that come to you. Stagnant water will soon smell and grow molds and bacteria. The strongest people aren't the people who win, but the people who don't give up when others thought they lost. *The race of life is not for the best but for the brave.* They are the ones who know that God has called them to success and nothing can stop that divine will.

Sometimes, God will place you in situations in which you have no natural gifting. In these cases, God puts you there to experience His power in order to accomplish your tasks. This is a season of character building.

Joseph went through a thirteen year season of character building and preparation for purpose. It was hardly an "assignment" that matched his purpose it might seem. But the process to fulfill his primary assignment included this painful process. This is how a young boy without a formal education could become a successful prime minister of Egypt.

Like I said earlier, most of the successful people we all recognize today didn't start out to be great or successful. They simply followed their passion and purpose. They either experienced problems in their personal lives or in the society that pulled out their purpose. Many of them were drafted into their larger story assignment because of a conflict or crisis. Consider Martin Luther, the Apostle Paul, Esther, King David, William Wilberforce, Martin Luther King – the list could go on. In each case they were thrust into a circumstance not of their choosing that led to their ultimate assignment in life that was rooted in their purpose. You cannot force that timetable. It is up to God when that time is just right.

Say No to lack

Poverty is evil and it's not of God. God has never intended for anyone to suffer or lack. The devil is the architect of everything evil. The devil created poverty. I know poverty first hand. I was born and raised in one of the African countries where most people lived below $2 a day. I saw many go without food for days. Children die due to malnutrition. Fathers disappeared because they couldn't provide for their own, mothers wept in despair as the milk ran out. I saw the evil of the lack of money with my own eye balls. The bible in Matthew 6:33 says, "Seek His kingdom first and everything you need will be provided to you." You cannot change the direction of your life, ministry or business until you change your daily focus from yourself unto God. Walking in prosperity and saying no to lack starts from putting God first. Receive the divine resources of heaven.

Ten benefits of discouragements

1. Forces you to seek God

There is nothing that draws us closer to God like discouragements do. When we'e discouraged, we have no one to turn to but God. King David said, *"From the end of the earth will I cry unto thee, when my heart is overwhelmed: lead me to the rock that is higher than I."* Psalms 61:2

2. Brings Clarity and renewed focus

Discouragements have an interesting way of narrowing our focus and bringing clarity to your purpose. A while back, I had some of my most loved church members come against me and really hurt our church. The disappointments helped me to focus on some new church members who love the church and love me.

3. Sign of success

Oh I like this one! When you feel discouraged it is actually because you are succeeding at something. Discouragements are not what we usually think they are. Discouragements are the symptoms of success and progress. When you are achieving purpose, discouragements come in to re-energize your potential.

4. Tests your convictions

Do you really believe what you say you believe? Do you believe what you think you believe? Don't be so quick to answer the questions until you have tasted the teas of adversities and discouragements. The strength of a tea is when it is in hot water. That is when what is on the inside shows. God will allow discouragement to come in to test your convictions in your purpose. DON'T QUIT. It's only a test!

5. Builds greater adaptation and flexibility

Discouragement matures and grows you faster than anything else does. You will learn how to control your emotions and adapt to the changes around you. Adaptation and flexibility are necessary tools in the school of success and accomplishments.

6. It releases greater creativity

When the walls seems like they are closing down on you and your options seem limited, it forces you to tap deeper into your creativity. This is creativities and ideas you never thought you had in you until you were forced to dig deeper. I want to encourage you right here, when discouragements come in, don't fret, don't give up. Dig deeper into the wisdom of God in you.

7. Takes focus off you and unto others

Sometimes we are so selfish and so focused on ourselves and yet don't even know it. The life of purpose is a life of serving and giving unto others and making the world a better and happier place. Sometimes God allows discouragements from the devil to set in to remind us to take our focus off ourselves and unto others. Jesus told us in the bible that He came not to be served but to serve.

8. Learn not to be a people pleaser
Let me say up front that people pleasers do not attain their purpose. Your purpose will offend some people. They will not like it or believe in it. To be significant and successful in your greatness you will have to be comfortable with people not liking you. Super successful achievers don't care much about what other people think about them.

9. Builds your strength and character
Gold gets better and more precious when it passes through the fire. The fire purifies it and gets the impurities out. The devil usually sends us discouragements to hinder us but God uses it to build our strength and character.

10. Final test before breakthrough happens
In my observations of life and success breakthroughs in different people over the years, I have noticed that discouragement sets in just at the moment when the breakthrough is just about to happen. Imagine with me for a minute, a farmer trying to bring down a tree. He understands that it is not the first hit that brings down the tree but the last one. So he perseveres until he sees the tree come down. That is how our attitude should be when we are in our expedition of purpose.

When God calls you to walk down a certain path, He gives you, and only you, the grace for that assignment. Do not let others sway you out of sympathy or reasoning. This is an important truth to embrace. Your calling is unique to you. Do not compare yourself to others or listen to counsel based on natural reasoning.

Destroy your fears

Barack Obama was born on August 4, 1961 in Honolulu, Hawaii to a Kenyan father and an American mother. He is the 44th and current President of the United States and the first African American to hold the office. When President Obama started consulting with people about running for President, some of his closest friends and family advised him against running for fear of being assassinated. Had he listened to them, he would have lost the battle of purpose. Sometimes our friends and families do not always know God's plan for our lives. We can't always surround ourselves with people that speak fear as a language but we need to mount ourselves with those that speak the language of faith. The Bible says, *"We walk by faith and not by sight."* 2 Corinthians 5:7

Fear is a robber of destinies. Fear has destroyed great dreams and dreamers. I have seen fear reduce the giants of men to midgets. General Colin Powell in my opinion could have been the first black president of America, but the fear of being assassinated prevented him from pursuing the high office. The ten spies missed out of Canaan and lost the battle of courage because they welcomed fear into their hearts. Joshua and Caleb ignored their fear and experienced the blessings of God. The Bible exposes fear as a tormentor. 1 John 4:18 *"There is no fear in love; but perfect love casts out fear, because fear involves torment. But he who fears has not been made perfect in love."*

Every disadvantage also has an advantage connected with it. You are the one that God has chosen for the task and God never made a mistake with your purpose. Go and shine!

Discussion Questions

1. Name one of the benefits of discouragements?

2. Who are some people who have inspired you that were labeled as disadvantaged?

3. What things can you do to overcome discouragement?

4. Can you name some abilities in your perceived disabilities?

5. What are some of the reasons why discouragements are necessary on the journey of purpose?

6. Can you think of a time in your life when you were discouraged about something that later became a blessing to you?

7. How do you plan to destroy fear in your life?

8. How do you plan to help other people out of their discouragement?

9. Name some of the abilities in you that are an advantage in your pursuit of purpose?

10. How would this new understanding regarding discouragement help you in decoding your purpose?

Chapter Ten
THE GREAT DISCOVERY

It is my deepest prayer that at this stage of this book, you're decoding and understanding God's divine idea for your existence and the solutions you are to bring to the world. This is the great discovery. The great discovery is when you begin to understand your calling and purpose on the earth. It is when you awaken from sleep to the sweet morning breeze of your purpose. When you discover something that you can put your whole life into, it will fill your life with excitement and purpose. It will give your life a meaning. When you decode your assignment on earth, it will give you fresh energy and passion. Apostle Paul wrote, *"Asking God, the glorious Father of our Lord Jesus Christ, to give you spiritual wisdom and insight so that you might grow in your knowledge of God"* James 1:17 NLT

Purpose is Specific

One of the main things about the divine idea for your purpose is that it is specific. God is not confused about what and who he created you to be and the problems you were born to solve. God's intention for your existence is precise to the dot. Allow me to take this a little deeper. It is not enough to understand that your purpose is to be a Doctor. What kind of a Doctor are you? Are you a surgeon? Are you a cardiologist? Or are you a neurologist? Learning the specificity of your assignment will save you a lot of time and energy. This will prevent you from running the rat race and chasing every passion you can cook up.

I understand that my general purpose is to be a preacher of the gospel but my specific purpose is to teach SUCCESS and PURPOSE principles to the world and take people to their higher place of destiny and purpose. I am so disciplined to my specific purpose and I work daily to hone and maximize my potentials. This book Purpose Decoded is my tenth book. Praise God! Out of the ten books I have written, I have never written a book on the Second Coming of Jesus, Holiness or Greek and Hebrews study of the bible because that is not my purpose to the body of Christ. I don't have any passion or energy towards any topic or issues that are outside my area of calling and purpose. This is one of the ways you can tell if you are in a Purpose-Malfunction state is when you are doing things that you have no energy, passion or excitement for. It is like doing things that you really hate but you have to do it for other considerations like financial or other reasons. Apostle Paul said, *"I have not yet reached my goal, and I am not perfect. But Christ has taken hold of me. So I keep on running and struggling to take hold of the prize. My friends, I don't feel that I have already arrived. But I forget what is behind, and I struggle for what is ahead. I run toward the goal, so that I can win the prize of being called to heaven."* Philippians 3:12-14 CEV

Don't allow PEOPLE to DRAFT or DRAG you into things that you are not ANOINTED for. Your ANOINTING does NOT FUNCTION when you are outside your PURPOSE. Stay in your area of calling and meaning and unexplainable success is on the way. Oh boy! That will preach!

Purpose is Unique

I travel around the world and speak at great churches and conferences. Sometimes I notice certain things that I like in different circles that I associate with and they resonated with me thus I'm often tempted to copy ideas from them and make it my own. I will admit that in the times past I am quick to copy it but as I have grown, matured and decoded my purpose I fully understand now that God's divine idea for my existence and success is so specific and unique to me. When I try to imitate others, I won't be fulfilling the specific purpose that God created me for and I will be unable to maximize my potential. If something resonates strongly with me, I will not imitate it but rather let it serve as inspiration to me and my cause. The apostle wrote, *"By his divine power, God has given us everything we need for living a godly life. We have received all of this by coming to know him, the one who called us to himself by means of his marvelous glory and excellence."* 2 Peter 1:3 NLT

You must be true to the way God coded you. The way you were wired is different from everybody else. Stay true to yourself and have fun. Lower your shoulders a little bit, relax your face and let the sun shine on you.

Purpose Decoded: *You will only be judged by what God created you to do and not by what He created somebody else to do.*

People's success of failure in life is not dependent on the color of your skin. Purpose is color blind. You can be white, black, green, brown or yellow. It doesn't matter. All that matters for your success is that you be in the center of God's will for your life. Don't be afraid of standing out. Be who you really are!

How to discover your purpose

Here are some tips that would help you in your great discovery:

1. **Go to the Manufacturer**
Can you remember a time when you bought an electronic gadget that you didn't know how to operate? Reading the manual was practically useless because it didn't help much. What you should do is to give the manufacturer a call and let them help you get your gadget working. It's the same thing with your purpose. God is your manufacturer. He coded and brought you into existence. He alone holds the key to your great discovery.

2. **Listen to your inner voice**
Now you have gone to your manufacturer and He is revealing to you the meaning of your life. He will tell you and reveal his divine purpose for you and the problems you were assigned to. Sometimes he will reveal your purpose all at once but most times He will reveal it to you sequentially with time. Listen to God in your inner voice, believe what He tells you and do it.

3. **Pay attention to your life**
This is perhaps one of the easiest ways you decode your purpose. Pay attention to your life. *Your purpose is screaming at you everywhere you turn.* The problems you are assigned to solve are begging you to answer their cry. What pain moves you? What passion motivates you? Whose cry is distinct in your ears? What would you do if no one ever paid you for it? What do you have incredible joy and excitement doing? What kinds of problems and opportunities always find their way to your space? Many

times your purpose has shown up in your door step over and over again but you have neglected to see it for what it is.

4. Use a purpose list
My wife likes to make lists for everything. She makes a list for groceries, the kid's morning rituals and for everything. Most of us are good list makers as well. But my question is, do you have a purpose list. A purpose list is one that itemizes your life goals, dreams and purpose. Do you have a place where you have written out your purpose, see it every day and be inspired by it? The bible says, *"Then the Lord answered me and said: "Write the vision and make it plain on tablets, That he may run who reads it."* Habakkuk 2:2

5. Speak to a mentor
Find a good mentor and learn from them. A good mentor will understand and help you to decode your purpose. I encourage you to ask them questions about your purpose. Don't be afraid to ask those questions that are on your heart and the ones that are bothering you. You may be surprised at the wisdom that comes forth.

6. Learn from your mistakes
Sometimes the game of life is like chess. Do not be afraid to make mistakes. When you make a move and you find out it is not the right move for you, don't quit, just pack your bags and head the other way. Discovering your purpose is a journey and not a destination. It might take a few efforts of trying for you to finally pin down your life purpose. Mistakes are not what we think they are. Mistakes are episodes of learning that should make us better.

7. Your Purpose is Not Always Tied to What You Do

Your job or career is not necessarily your purpose. Because you are enjoying your job and bringing in a decent salary and check doesn't mean you are in purpose. I have met a lot of preachers of the gospel turn to business when the times are hard for them. That is another example of Purpose-Malfunction. Your purpose will always provide opportunity for you. Stay in it. Don't run from it. Put a demand on it to produce for you so can remain relevant.

7. Your purpose is clear and simple

If you cannot state your purpose in 30 seconds or less then you don't really know what it is. If you cannot tell someone God's divine idea for your existence in less than 20 minutes that's a problem. Your purpose should be so clear, simple and concise that you can state it in 20 seconds or less. Your purpose might be a phrase instead of a sentence. For example, the purpose of our church that I pastor is: *taking you to a higher place.*

8. The power of one thing

Your purpose is the one thing that you are supposed to give all of your time, energy and resources to accomplishing. History shows us that men and women that accomplished their purpose on earth were those that were focused on one thing instead of allowing themselves to be derailed and distracted by many things. Whether it was Moses, Nehemiah, Joshua, Esther, Martin Luther King, Ghandi, Nelson Mandela or Thomas Edison; they all understood the power of one thing. Your purpose is the one thing that you were born to do. Allow God to reveal it to do today and your life will never be the same.

9. Check the provision

This is one of the great tests of purpose. God will fund what He sponsors. When you are in purpose, you will enjoy God's provision and blessing. God's provision is a sign of His approval on what you are doing.

Pastor Rick Warren wrote a mega block buster book a few years ago that sold over 30 million copies called "The Purpose Driven Life" where he wrote that: "Many people try to use God for their own self-actualization, but that is a reversal of nature and it is doomed to failure. You were made for God, not vice versa, and life is about letting God use you for his purposes, not using him for your own purpose." Jesus said, *"In the same way, let your good deeds shine out for all to see, so that everyone will praise your heavenly Father."* Matthew 5:16 (NLT)

God will provide for you when you are in purpose.

Decoding Purpose – Transmission intercepted

Purpose and problems go together. Problems are an opportunity for purpose. If there was not the problem of Saul disobeying God, David would not have come into his full purpose to be king. Even giants in our lives help us to shine through into our purpose. They help us to focus and dig deeper to pull out what was hidden within us all along.

A Christian that is driven by purpose makes a difference at church and everywhere they go. We are called to be difference makers. Pastors should teach their members on how to live on purpose, managers should train their employees to be purposeful in their service to the company. When everyone is purposeful, the world is a better place just like God imagined it to be.

Discussion Questions

1. What is your purpose statement in one sentence?

2. What are some things that you are great at?

3. What is the one thing that you need to be investing your time, energy and resources into?

4. Based on the definition of Purpose-Malfunction, what are the things you are doing that is an example of Purpose-Malfunction?

5. What is God saying to you about your purpose right now?

6. When you pay attention to your life, what does it tell you about your purpose?

7. Do you think the provision of God matches your purpose right now?

8. Do you have a purpose list? If not, why so?

9. Name the people in your life that you trust to help you to decode your purpose?

10. What has been your greatest discovery thus far?

Chapter Eleven
PURPOSE, VISION AND SUCCESS

You can gain valuable insights into your purpose by looking at the things you can't stop doing. When you're immersed in these activities you're likely to lose track of time. You enjoy it so much that you even forget to eat and take a shower. You don't think about what you're doing. You just do it. It's like you are in "a zone" and you don't want to let out. Anyone that interrupts you in the zone can be a victim of your rage. I am sure you know what I am talking about. In this chapter I want to teach you about the power of vision.

The realization of your purpose is tied to the largeness of your vision. Imagine with me a nice automobile, maybe an Orange Bentley with blue chrome wheels. That is a beautiful car. I will buy it if I find one. The car is beautiful but it cannot function or maximize its purpose without Gasoline. It is not useful without gasoline. It aint going nowhere without gasoline even though it is a beautifully made exotic and expensive car. It's the same way with vision and purpose. Without a God sized vision for your life, you are like that Orange Bentley with blue chrome wheels without gasoline. Your purpose, life vision and success are all associated. Your vision gives life to your purpose.

Vision comes from Purpose

When an ELEPHANT is ANGRY the Forest SUFFERS. You're an Elephant and not a Mosquito. You were born to be LARGE. Your largeness is equivalent to the vision of your purpose. Before God creates anything, the first thing He does is to have a clear vision for it. God starts with an idea or vision before He creates anything. Then he assigns a purpose to that vision. Every time in the scriptures that God created anything or used anybody for a divine assignment; the first thing He does is to give them a Divine vision. This was the case with Abraham. The book of Genesis records *"And the Lord said to Abram, after Lot had separated from him: "Lift your eyes now and look from the place where you are—northward, southward, eastward, and westward; for all the land which you see I give to you and your descendants forever."* Genesis 13: 14-15

Humans are very visual. *God knows that it is difficult for a person to deny what they saw.* A person might deny what they heard but it is hard for them to deny what they saw with their own eyes or experienced. This is why our experiences are very powerful in shaping our personality and purpose. So what God does is to give you a new vision for your life that is far grandiose than what you have ever experienced before. Seeing this vision one or two times will not change your life. You need to stay in the vision long enough until you have an unshakable memory and experience from it. The VISION has to become your CONVICTION. Hold on to what God showed you with passion and conviction! Don't lose hold of the vision for your life. Vision is the guarantee of purpose.

Purpose Decoded: *Vision energizes your purpose.*

Apostle John rightly states, *"That which was from the beginning, which we have heard, which we have seen with our eyes, which we have looked upon, and our hands have handled, concerning the Word of life— the life was manifested, and we have seen, and bear witness, and declare to you that eternal life which was with the Father and was manifested to us— that which we have seen and heard we declare to you, that you also may have fellowship with us; and truly our fellowship is with the Father and with His Son Jesus Christ. And these things we write to you that your joy may be full."*
1 John 1:1-4

Purpose Assignment: I invite you to take a blank sheet of paper and make a list of all the things you can't stop doing. Then ask your friends and colleagues (Purpose Partners) for help with this assignment. They will have noticed some that you may have overlooked. Sometimes people around us can sense our purpose faster than we can comprehend it. Believe in your purpose, believe in your greatness. To help you get started, here are some of mine:

- Can't stop writing books…lol (10 so far in less than 7 years)
- Can't stop talking about God's plan for your purpose and success
- Can't stop loving on people. (Even though I have been hurt a lot)
- Can't stop helping people to accomplish their dreams and purpose
- Can't stop helping people to develop a new business, book, film or make their ideas come to pass
- Can't stop thinking that there's a Divine idea for your existence and Success

Vision gives Direction

Visualization or "Seeing" is the act of imagining compelling and vivid pictures, ideas or expected realities in your mind or heart of what you want in your life. It may be the most underutilized purpose tool that you possess. When you consistently visualize your purpose coming to pass you release God's creative powers to work for you to bring it to pass.

Don't roam about in life aimlessly. Where there's no clear direction, there can be no progress. You need to locate direction for your life by vision. You are destined to be a star.

You will never become a star until you become a visionary. Copying another person's vision reduces you from a *Star* to a *Scar*.

Referees in a game, and even spectators do not receive any trophy after a football final; so don't be one. *No press no prize*. The bible says, *"There is a way that seems right to a person, but eventually it ends in death."* Proverbs 14:12 GW

Vision is the source of life. It's God language in communicating to us. Vision shapes the world. Real vision transcends time and present conditions. It is the secret of the great and mighty and without vision people perish- they never attain to purpose!

Purpose Decoded: *A life without vision is an empty life.*

A person devoid of a vision for their life, marriage, family or business merely exists- this person is going no where. Getting a vision is one of the essentials in decoding your purpose. It is the foundation upon which the other purpose essentials are built. Vision is the greatest power that God has given to humankind to utilize in creating their life and the world. I guarantee you that your life will remarkably change when you realize the magnificent vision that God has for your life.

You must have a big vision for your life. It has to be so unbelievably humongous that it scares everyone around you including you.

Purpose Decoded: *No army, no police, no demonic power can stop a person with a vision.*

What you see is what you get

The muscle movement that helps us to physically take action in our lives begins in the mind. Mind matters! That is why all great golfers, soccer stars, tennis players, basketball players, and the like, visualize themselves making a shot beforehand. An experiment conducted by Alan Richardson, an Australian psychologist, found that improvements in performance increased 23% among those subjects who visualized everyday for 20 days. In his paper published in *Research Quarterly*, Richardson wrote that the most effective visualization occurs when the visualizer feels and sees what he is doing. You can be successful on your own terms doing what you really love. The power of vision can't be overstated. It's the antidote to attaining life's maximum.

Mary Youngblood was a welfare mum turned Grammy Award Winner. On a recent interview, she discussed how her life was transformed: "I really visualized it, too, even as a child watching those programs. I could visualize myself walking up the stage, up the stairs. For me, visualizing those dreams happening was pertinent to making that happen, because I could see it. I pictured it in my head."

Allow me to share a story with you. On a Wednesday

evening; my phone rang. Ring ring ring! Julie was on the line. The moment I said "Hello" I knew something was wrong by the grunt in her voice. "What's going on with you" I inquired.

"I got jilted again" was her remorseful response.

"It seems no man wants me" she continued. She was 35 years old and had experienced numerous break-ups in her lifetime. My next question shocked her a bit:

"Julie, do you have a vision for your life?" I asked her.

"What's your vision for your Purpose Mate?" The words hurried out of my mouth like a loaded machine gun. Her voice lightening up, she confirmed to me that she doesn't have a vision for her life or life partner. I explained that was the cause of her continued dilemma and proceeded to coach her. She was very receptive and continued to listen attentively. I gave her a vision assignment.

I told her to visualize and write on paper, ten things or qualities that she wants to see in her vision husband, then stick the paper on her mirror where she would see it daily; and then prophesy it, which is "Say it" out of her mouth daily.

She started seeing it in her imagination and saying it out of her mouth almost daily. She wanted her purpose-mate to be 6 feet tall, a committed Christian man, dark and handsome and have a job. Then four months later, Julie called me again and this time with a thunderous joy in her voice. She had just started dating a guy that met all ten qualities she wrote on her vision board. He had proposed, cooks for her, washes her car, gives her fifteen year old a monthly allowance. She could hardly contain herself, saying to me, "the vision assignment worked, I know that this is my husband." The previous guys she dated didn't score more than three, when compared to her vision board.

"When you want to lead, start with the future." Buckingham said. "Get specific. And get vivid."

It is already done

One of the most powerful aspects of vision is that vision sees something as if it is already done. Your purpose was completed before you were formed in your mother's womb. When you understand this truth it shall set you free. It shall set you free from worry, fear, anxiety and panic attacks. You will understand that your life has been laid out for you to come and enjoy and touch lives and make the world a happier place. Jesus said, *"Then you will know the truth, and the truth will set you free."* John 8:32 NIV

I'd like to remind you that God shaped you to solve specific troubles for mankind. The earth will not be the same without your existence. You are truly SUCCESSFUL when you are in PURPOSE. *Catch this divine idea for your being and live it to the optimal possibility.*

Have you seen the vision of what is possible with your purpose? There is no limit to who you can be or what you can do. The power to accomplish your vision, dreams and purpose is already inside of you, waiting for you to awaken to your true calling.

Dream bigger and larger than you have ever been, set a course for your life and make it happen. The whole universe is waiting for you.

Please close your eyes wherever you (if it is safe to do so) and dream as far, wide and deep as you can! Release that glorious vision that God is showing you out of your mouth.

Discussion Questions

1. What can't you stop doing?

2. How will you incorporate time to visualize the vision for your life into your day?

3. What is the vision for your life, marriage, family and business?

4. What's making you dream small dreams?

5. How does Purpose and Vision correlate each other?

6. Make a vision list of the top 10 things you want to accomplish with your life. What are they?

7. Why do you think many people are not dreaming big visions?

8. How can vision help us to stay focused in our purpose?

9. When was the last time you shared your vision with your purpose partners?

10. What is the greatest thing you learned from this chapter?

Chapter Twelve
PURPOSE AND PROVISION

You were coded for first class living. When I understood clearly that God's provision for my life, ministry, and business is tied to my purpose I did a happy dance. It instantly paralyzed all fears and concerns about my financial wellbeing. I stopped being concerned about being able to fund and provide for my family. I got it that God will never sponsor a project that He wouldn't pay for. *My existence was never my idea, it was God's idea.* He brought you and I into this world for His vision for the earth. Wouldn't you think He will provide for His own plan? Of course he would!

I've counseled many people that are not successful and not fulfilled in their lives. Almost every time I probe deeper I find a commonality amongst them all. They're expecting the provisions of God when they are not in their **Place of Purpose.** There is a place called "there." That is your place of Purpose.

Your place of purpose is your assignment, including the geographical location of your assignment

In the Old Testament God taught Abraham about provisions. One day the voice of God spoke to him to go and offer his only son Isaac as a sacrifice on Mount Moriah. Abraham quickly obeyed God and took his boy to slaughter to God as a burnt sacrifice. But when they got to the place of sacrifice, the young boy Isaac noticed that there was wood, a knife but no ram for the sacrifice. Isaac wasn't privy to the conversation between God and his father Abraham.

His father Abraham, was a man of faith and purpose. He knew and understood God's purpose for his life. Abraham replied Isaac, "My son, God will provide for Himself the lamb for a burnt offering."

Provision Consciousness

I am trying to re-educate your mind about God's provisions for your life. I want you to start seeing the provisions of God all around you. At every phase and season in your journey of purpose, please know that God puts in place adequate provisions for each of those phases and seasons.

You might ask, "Dr. Abraham, if there are God's provisions all around me, then why am I not seeing them?

That's a good question. The problem is not the provision; it is what you are seeing. You have to look with the eyes of FAITH and see with your SPIRIT your provisions.

When Abraham told Isaac that God will provide there was no physical ram around that vicinity. But Abraham saw the ram with his spirit eyes and when he opened his natural eyes the ram was there.

Sometimes you have to close your physical eyes so that your spiritual eyes can help you to decode the provisions for your purpose and assignment. I will come back to the Abraham story later; I also remember a story that Dr. David Yonggi Cho shared in his book, "The Fourth Dimension." There was time that his church was very small and yet he decoded God's purpose and saw that he was supposed to be an international mega church pastor. He began to employ the visualization of his dreams and purpose just like I have taught you in the previous chapter. He said he would close his eyes and start preaching to his congregation. According to him, he was training his physical eyes to align with his spiritual eyes. Dr. Cho found out that when he uses his physical eyes the place is small and his members are few, but when he closes his physical eyes and opens his spiritual eyes, he sees the hall packed full and thousands of people in his church hearing his messages. Today Dr. David Yonggi Cho is living his purpose and his church is currently the largest single church congregation with over 750,000 members.

Just Look

Go tap somebody on their shoulder and say, "Just look." In continuation of the story I was sharing with you earlier about Abraham. After the conversation exchange with Isaac, Abraham tied his son on the altar he built and was ready to offer him as a burnt sacrifice unto the Lord. As he lowered his hand to kill Isaac, the angel of God spoke to him and said, "Abraham, look behind you." When Abraham looked he saw the ram that God had provided for the burnt offering from the very beginning.

I would like for you to put a budget together for that dream in your heart, and I want you to believe that God has already provided for it. When it seems like all is bleak, Just look. There is a ram of provision tied somewhere just waiting for you to show up.

Before you think of the plan, God already thought of the provision. I know that might sound cheap but it is so true. God had planned out your purpose. Your purpose is not your personal undertaking, it's God's divine idea for your existence.

God is not a SCIENTIST, so you are not an EXPERIMENT! Oh boy! That will preach! You were not born to merely exist but to live out a set divine plan.

The concept of purpose and provisions is so transformational. Like I said earlier, God has better things to do than to create you to fail or live out a mediocre, unexciting and fruitless life. God doesn't waste His time and so He didn't waste His time forming you and coding your purpose. Wake up from the shackles that have hindered your sense of purpose and identity.

In this chapter, I want you to be conscious of God's provision all around you. **The money you need to start that new business is already provided.** All you have to do is to look and you will see your ram tied up and waiting for you to just look.

Don't be afraid to follow your dreams and passions because of monetary or societal pressures. Do not rob your generation of your purpose. Think of it this way, there are countless lives that are counting on you and for your purpose to be decoded so that they can be blessed.

All the money in the world is yours

I might not know the specifics of your purpose but I do know that God's plans for your life included financial provisions. All the money in the world is yours. I hear a conversation in heaven, when God created you and planted you in your mother's womb via your Dad's sperm, he called goodness, mercy and money to accompany you on your journey to earth. You didn't come alone. You were accompanied by all that you needed. Apostle Paul wrote, *"For the earnest expectation of the creature waiteth for the manifestation of the sons of God."* Romans 8:19

Your purpose is much more important than individual goals. It's the direction that's right for you. Your purpose arises from your talents and your values. It's like the horizon. You can pursue your purpose for the rest of your life.

Living on purpose, as I define it, is to become aware that we were all created to serve some specific function in life. Some of these purposes might be lofty, attracting the accolades of the world. Some of these purposes may be down-to-earth, such as raising a child, teaching or engaging in some other activity that may not be as acknowledged by society but is still significant.

Stop trying to be who you are not

My final thought on the area of Purpose and Provision is another epidemic that is out there. It's when people are trying to be who they are not. They either ignore or are condescending of their divine purpose and so they just try to be something that appears glamorous. They want to be "number one" where as they purpose is to be "number two." Similar to when someone is trapped in a suit that is not theirs. When you stay within the confines of your purpose, you will be amazed at the way that God will bless you. You will be amazed on the amount of blessings and provisions that will overflow in your life and push you into your purpose. **No matter how small your purpose appears to be, in it is enough provisions for you for a lifetime.** There is provisions for you my friend and it is hidden in your purpose.

Discussion Questions

1. Why is it important to be who you are?

2. Is there any reason why you are not seeing your provision?

3. What do you need to start visualizing about?

4. What did you think the author meant when he said, "Sometimes you need to close your physical eyes so that you can see with your spiritual eyes?"

5. Does the size of the provision you need to accomplish your purpose intimidate you?

6. "God is not a Scientist, so you're not an experiment." What do you understand by that statement?

7. Why is it important to be generous to your church?

8. How can you develop Provision Consciousness?

9. Why is provision connected to your purpose?

10. What would you do with your life if you knew that God has deposited all the provision you needed into your bank account?

Chapter Thirteen
RELEASING YOUR PURPOSE

Wow! You've made it to the end of the book. I believe God that your life is changed and you have decoded your purpose. Congratulations to you! Yes, you did it!

In this final chapter, all you have to do is to release and unleash your purpose to the world. Your purpose is found in the specific problems that God created you to solve. This divine idea for your existence is so exciting and enriching to all that come in contact with you. Jesus said, *"You are the light of the world—like a city on a hilltop that cannot be hidden. No one lights a lamp and then puts it under a basket. Instead, a lamp is placed on a stand, where it gives light to everyone in the house. In the same way, let your good deeds shine out for all to see, so that everyone will praise your heavenly Father."* Matthew 5:14-16 NLT

Don't minimize your purpose

Your purpose may look small in your eyes but it is mighty in the eyes of God. Don't underestimate the reason you were born. You are capable of accomplishing great things in your life. Dream a big dream and go out and do it. God is setting you up for a mighty breakthrough. The test of perseverance is the one that many people cannot endure. All too often, they will move when God tells them to be still and wait. They will decide that they have been waiting long enough, so they set out to deliver themselves. This is a big mistake. If God has not completed the deeper work in you, He will take you around the mountain one more time-or even more if that is what is necessary to complete the inner work that He has begun in your life. The bible says, *"For in him we live and move and have our being.' As some of your own poets have said, 'We are his offspring.'"* Acts 17:28 NIV

Purpose and Passion

You were never made or expected by God to solve every problem or to be everything to everyone. You were created by God to be the solution to some precise problems. Everything that God made was with the intention to solve a problem and add value to the existing situation or environment. "God never gave anyone everything but he gave everyone something." Bishop T.D. Jakes

Purpose Decoded: *Decoding your purpose prevents you from robbing your world with your beautiful existence*

Your purpose is already completed in God

Everyone wants to know their purpose in life. They want to understand what they were put on earth to do. It is good to know that God finishes a product in the spirit before He begins to manufacture it. *Your beginning is an evidence of your completion.* I have to remind you again that your purpose was completed before you started it. Make heaven proud of you. *A life out of purpose is a penniless life.* The day you understand purpose is the day of your great discovery. That's when you awaken out of slumber and start living. Merely existing is cheating your world out of your existence. Saturate the world with your purpose and your entrance into the world.

How to release your purpose

Decoding your purpose is the first in achieving it. The second step is to release it. Here are four steps that would help you to release God's purpose for your life:

1. Believe in your purpose

God's purpose for our lives is always larger than our biggest dreams and aspirations. His divine idea for our existence is so gigantic that it often leaves us wondering in our thoughts if we could ever attain and satisfy it. But I want to tell you that it is doable. God will never give you more than you can handle. He will never leave or forsake us. You cannot live out a purpose that you don't believe in. If God calls you a billionaire, you have to believe that's who you are.

When God first revealed his purpose for Moses to be the deliverer of His people, Moses objected to it. He felt he was incapable and under qualified for the enormous task. He told God to use someone else because he was a stutterer. What Moses didn't understand at the time is that God had already made plans and provisions for Moses concerns. God knew he was a stutterer and yet he decided to use him to be his spokesman to Pharaoh.

Have faith in God's ability to accomplish great things through you. Stop undermining yourself as being insignificant. God never made anything that was insignificant. Your life is greater than you see right now. Believe in your purpose, believe in your dreams and believe in yourself. Receive the grace and anointing to function in your purpose. The bible says, *"For as he thinks in is heart, so is he..."* Proverbs 23:7

2. Obey the law of crazy instructions

Crazy instructions are those commands from the Lord that don't make any natural, academic, scientific or human sense; yet necessary to accomplish God's dream for your life and purpose. Whenever God speaks to you, act on it. He knows more about your purpose than you understand about it. He created your purpose and He knows how to lead you in it. All you have to do is to follow his leadings, voice and instructions especially when it doesn't make any sense.

I remember in 2010, God told my wife and I to relocate from Dallas, Texas to Atlanta, Georgia. It was a crazy instruction because we were comfortable in Dallas, Texas at the time. We lived there for six years. I married my beautiful wife in Dallas and we had two children at the time, a thriving young church, businesses and my wife was a professor at a local college. Everything seemed fine, except that I wasn't fulfilled. It seem like my dreams were not fully manifesting in Dallas. I felt like something was amiss but couldn't really figure out what it was. Dr. Faith and I knew we had to leave Dallas but didn't know where to go. I wanted to go somewhere I had never been before and where I didn't know anybody. I didn't want to be comfortable again. I knew I had to rely on God completely or I would perish. It's been almost five years, at the time of this writing and since we obeyed that crazy instruction from the Lord and we have since many of our dreams fulfilled effortlessly and now we are living in purpose.

God wants to speak to you. He has so much to

communicate to you. Sadly many people believe that hearing God's voice is the exclusive reserve of a few special people. That is not true. God wants to speak to you everyday. It is not difficult to hear God's voice. I will show you in this chapter how you can hear God's voice everyday so that you can win the battle of crazy instructions. Jesus said, *"And when he brings out his own sheep, he goes before them; and the sheep follow him, for they know his voice."* John 10:4

God spoke to the Prophets of old, He's still speaking today. The book of Exodus records, *"And God spoke to Moses and said to him: "I am the Lord."* Exodus 6:2

God instructed Noah to build an ark (boat ship) so that he, his family, animals and all those that will respond to his voice would escape the flood that was about to destroy the earth. The problem is that Noah had never seen rain or a flood before, because prior to the flood, God irrigated the earth from the ground up. Another problem was that Noah had never built an ark before which is in the form of a big ship. But Noah didn't complain or make excuses. He trusted God and obeyed the crazy instruction he was given. Sometimes the voice of God doesn't make natural sense, yet when we follow and obey His voice, we are led to a life of victory and abundance.

Trusting God means having faith to believe that He knows what is best for you, your family, business and career. The Bible says, *"But without faith it is impossible to please him: for he that cometh to God must believe that he is, and that he is a rewarder of them that diligently seek him."* Hebrews 11:6

How to Hear God's Voice
Hearing the voice of God is the greatest security for Significance and living out your purpose. Here are a few tips that will help

you to hear the voice of God more clearly and begin to fulfill those crazy instructions:

1. **Build an intimate relationship with the Holy Spirit.** This means, spending time with Him everyday, singing and making melodies in your heart to the Lord. The more you spend time with someone the more distinct their voice will be to you. Read Ephesians 5:18-20.

2. **Feast on the Word.** The word of God is God. The word reveals the character of God. The more time you spend in the word, the more familiar you will be with the voice of the spirit. Be in love with the bible. Read Acts 20:32, John 1:1-14.

3. **Get into neutral.** This means you free yourself from all preconceived ideas and plans. It's hard to hear the voice of God when you already have your mind made up concerning a situation. Read Philippians 4:6-9.

4. **Confidence.** You'll have to have confidence in your own ability to hear from God. Without confidence, you will keep doubting and guessing if God is the one speaking to you. Have the confidence that God wants to clearly speak to you and you have the ability to hear His voice. Read Daniel 11:32, Hebrews 10:35.

5. **Follow the peace and promptings of your heart.** God will often speak to you through His peace. When you don't feel the complete peace of God in your heart about a certain situation; that may be a clue that God is trying to alert you about something. Also pay attention to the prompting and impressions in your heart. God speaks to us through that as well. You may not always hear an audible voice of God but you can feel his prompting and impressions in your spirit. Read Hebrews 12:14.

3. Speak out your purpose

The third step in releasing your purpose is to prophesy it. You've got to speak it out of your mouth almost on a daily basis. When you prophesy your purpose, you are agreeing with God and activating and mobilizing angels and heavenly hosts to work behind the scenes to actualize your purpose.

David had already defeated Goliath through his words even before the battle began. David understood that words have power and our mouths can release prophecies into our future. David said to Saul, *"Your servant has killed both lion and bear; and this uncircumcised Philistine will be like one of them, seeing he has defied the armies of the living God."* 1 Samuel 17:36

David said, 'this Goliath is going to die just like the lion and bear before him.' He was prophesying the outcome of the combat even before it began. That's the power of prophecy. He declared victory even before he threw the sling at Goliath.

Purpose Decoded: *A prophecy is a bold prediction of the future.*

A prophecy means that you are calling those things that be not as though they are. You are looking at an empty bank account and prophesying it full. You might be struggling to pay your bills, yet you have the audacity to say, "Someday I will be a multi millionaire." These are examples of practical prophecy.

We need to understand that our words carry prophetic power. It carries an inherent power that cannot be subdued. When you say constructive things, those things begin to happen to you. Likewise when you open your mouth and you say negative things, those negative things happen to you. It's not by chance nor is it by coincidence; it's because of what you have opened your mouth to say. Where do you see yourself 10 years from now? Start talking about it now.

Words Create Your World

I have always recognized the power of words and I tend to use them creatively. Words create our world. If we're too busy saying how sick people make us feel, how our job is killing us, how hard it is to find a good mate or how bad our nerves are; our world will never be what God intends for it to be. We should prosper in all things and be in health even as our soul prospers.

Purpose Decoded: *Speak Life. Speak change. Speak your new level.*

You can never attain purpose talking like a pauper. Great people don't talk small talk. People with great destinies stand out in the crowd because they speak vision not their fears. Speak out your purpose daily until you see it come to pass.

Don't Be Silent

God didn't create anyone or anything to be silent. Everyday somebody is saying something. But what are you saying? When the wind blows you can hear the sound of leaves- that is leaves talking, mountains erupt in volcanoes, birds hum and sing, the sea roars, the sky thunders; these are examples of living and non- living things that make noise. Everything was created to express itself in some form of articulate language. If they fail to do so, they will lose their right to exist. Likewise we as humans, we are expressive by nature. We are made in the image and likeness of God, the scripture tells us.

You are not an ordinary person. You have creative ability in you. You are an expression of God's divinity. An extraordinary being! Lift your head high. There are seeds of greatness inside of you. Speak it!

4. Act on it

Life is too short to sit down and do nothing with your purpose. There's not enough time to sit around and do nothing spectacular with your life. *You're on a mission with God. You're on a mission for God.* You're on a mission to change the world.

The scripture says, *"The created world itself can hardly wait for what's coming next."* Romans 8:19 MSG

Make up your mind to die empty. Decide to use every gift, talent, idea and skill that God gave you for the glory of His name and the betterment of your world.

The nations are waiting for you to rise up and solve the problems that you were born to do. *I want to encourage you to read this book at least twice so you can get all the riches contained within and put to action what you have read.* Sometimes it's just a word, a phrase or sentence that changes our lives. Allow this book to do that for you. Share this book with others; show them how they can get copies for themselves.

Purpose Makers *are those who change the world!* They know that their lives have no meaning until the live out their purpose. I'd like to continue this conversation with you on a special page set up at www.UyiAbraham.com/PurposeMakers.html
Congratulations!
You've found meaning!
The world is blessed because you were born!

137

Discussion Questions

1. How do you hear the voice of God?

2. What is your biggest take away from this chapter?

3. What things will help you to release your purpose?

4. Why is it necessary to act on your purpose?

5. How many times a day will you prophesy your purpose?

6. How often do you sing to the Lord and spend time in His word?

7. What are your biggest hindrances to releasing your purpose?

8. If you don't release your purpose, who will suffer from your inaction?

9. What will you start you doing today so you can die empty?

10. How has this book helped you in your journey of purpose?

Connect with me and others
@
PURPOSE MAKERS
COACHING NETWORK

For Dreamers,
Ministers,
Inventors,
Entrepreneurs,

Leaders,
Pastors,
Five Fold,
World Changers.

Toll Free: 1 888 537 5315

www.UyiAbraham.com

Thank you for reading my book,
I pray that it changed your life like it did mine!
I have other resources such as books, DvDs, Cds
that might interest you as well.

For speaking engagements and itinerary

Visit @

www.UyiAbraham.com

www.ingramcontent.com/pod-product-compliance
Lightning Source LLC
Chambersburg PA
CBHW060835050426
42453CB00008B/700